AS/A-LEVEL YEAR 1

STUDENT GUIDE

EDEXCEL

Psychology

Biological psychology and learning theories

Christine Brain

A ... COMPANY

Philip Allan, an imprint of Hodder Education, an Hachette UK company, Blenheim Court, George Street, Banbury, Oxfordshire OX16 5BH

Orders

Bookpoint Ltd, 130 Park Drive, Milton Park, Abingdon, Oxfordshire OX14 4SB

tel: 01235 827827

fax: 01235 400401

e-mail: education@bookpoint.co.uk

Lines are open 9.00 a.m.–5.00 p.m., Monday to Saturday, with a 24-hour message answering service. You can also order through the Hodder Education website: www.hoddereducation.co.uk

ISBN 978-1-4718-4366-2

First printed 2015

Impression number 5 4 3 2 1

Year 2019 2018 2017 2016 2015

This Guide has been written specifically to support students preparing for the Edexcel AS and A-level Psychology examinations. The content has been neither approved nor endorsed by Edexcel and remains the sole responsibility of the author.

Typeset by Integra Software Services Pvt. Ltd., Pondicherry, India

Cover photo: agsandrew/Fotolia

Printed in Italy

Hachette UK's policy is to use papers that are natural, renewable and recyclable products and made from wood grown in sustainable forests. The logging and manufacturing processes are expected to conform to the environmental regulations of the country of origin.

Contents

Content Guidance

The role of the central nervous system and neurotransmitters in human behaviour • The effects of recreational drugs on the transmission process in the central nervous system • The structure of the brain and human aggression • The role of evolution and natural selection to explain human behaviour including aggression • The role of hormones to explain human behaviour such as aggression • The psychodynamic explanation for aggression • Individual differences • Developmental psychology • Method • Studies • Key question • Practical investigation • Issues and debates (A-level only)

Classical conditioning • Operant conditioning • Social learning • Phobias: acquisition, maintenance, treatments • Individual differences • Developmental psychology • Method • Studies • Key question • Practical investigation • Issues and debates (A-level only)

Questions & Answers

Overview • Content • Method (also A-level Paper 3) • Studies • Key question • Practical investigation • Issues and debates (A-level only, Papers 1 and 3)

Overview • Content • Method (also A-level Paper 3) • Studies • Key question • Practical investigation • Issues and debates (A-level only, Papers 1 and 3)

■ Getting the most from this book

Exam tips

Advice on key points in the text to help you learn and recall content, avoid pitfalls, and polish your exam technique in order to boost your grade.

Knowledge check

Rapid-fire questions throughout the Content Guidance section to check your understanding.

Knowledge check answers

1 Turn to the back of the book for the Knowledge check answers.

Summaries

■ Each core topic is rounded off by a bullet-list summary for quick-check reference of what you need to know.

Exam-style questions

Commentary on the questions

Tips on what you need to do to gain full marks, indicated by the icon 🄴

Sample student answers

Practise the questions, then look at the student answers that follow.

Questions & Answers

(a) The test was found not to be significant at p ≤0.05. Explain what this means. [2 marks]

🄴 There are 2 points-based AO2 marks. The question is about levels of significance. Explain what the phrase p≤0.05 means and what it means to say that the study is not significant at that level. 'Explain' requires you to give the point and then justify/link it to the study.

Student answer

p ≤ 0.05 means that the probability that the results are due to chance is equal to or less than 5%. ✓ Saying that the results are not significant at that level means there is a greater than 5% probability of the results being due to chance so the null hypothesis would not be rejected. ✓ p ≤ 0.05 is the most generous level of significance where results are accepted in psychology.

🄴 2/2 marks awarded. This gains the marks as the answer shows clear understanding of the 5% level of significance and what it means to say that level is not achieved.

Studies

(1) Describe the aims of Watson and Rayner (1920) and one study from Becker et al. (2002), Bastian et al. (2011) or Capafóns et al. (1998). [4 marks]

🄴 There are 4 points-based AO1 marks. The question focuses on the classic study in learning theories and one of the three contemporary studies. Be ready to pick out the study you have learned about, and not to be put off by seeing named studies you may not know about. The aims are what the researchers set out to achieve. As there are 2 marks for each study's aims, you need to write quite a bit in each case.

Student answer

Watson and Rayner (1920) carried out what is known as the Little Albert study. The aim was to see if the principles of classical conditioning could be used to give a phobia in a human baby. ✓ They wanted to condition the baby to fear what he had previously enjoyed playing with. Becker et al. (2002) carried out a study in Fiji. They wanted to look at the role of the media, specifically television, on eating behaviour, to test the claim that observational learning can take place. ✓ They aimed to use Fiji girls as participants, just as television was being introduced, and to ask them about their attitudes to eating and food and then to ask them 3 years later to see if their attitudes had changed — as well as finding out about their television watching habits. They wanted to see if watching television and having television role models would affect their attitudes to diet and eating. ✓

🄴 3/4 marks awarded. This answer has a lot of information. However, the second sentence about the Watson and Rayner (1920) study is not quite detailed or different enough from the first to get a second mark. A second sentence could be added, such as: 'They wanted to condition the baby to fear what he had previously enjoyed playing with. Specifically they wanted to see if causing fear by striking a

Commentary on sample student answers

Find out how many marks each answer would be awarded in the exam and then read the comments (preceded by the icon 🄴) following each student answer. Annotations that link back to points made in the student answers show exactly how and where marks are gained or lost.

■About this book

This guide covers two topic areas of the Edexcel AS and A-level Psychology specifications: Topic 3 Biological psychology and Topic 4 Learning theories, examined in AS Paper 2 and A-level Papers 1 and 3.

Table 1 shows how these three papers fit in the overall AS and A-level qualifications.

AS	A-level year 1	A-level year 2
Paper 1: social, cognitive	Paper 1: social, cognitive, **biological, learning** (including issues and debates)	Paper 2: clinical and one from criminological, child and health (including issues and debates)
Paper 2: **biological, learning**	Paper 3: **psychological skills** (method, studies, issues and debates)	

Table 1 Overview of AS and A-level papers (**bold** indicates topics covered in this guide)

Aims

This guide is not a textbook — there is no substitute for reading and taking notes. Nor does it tell you the actual questions on your paper. The aim of this guide is to give a clear understanding of the requirements of AS Paper 2 and A-level Papers 1 and 3, and to advise you on how best to meet these requirements. This guide looks at:

- the psychology you need to know about
- what you need to be able to do and what skills you need
- how you could go about learning the necessary material
- what is being examined, including mathematical skills
- how you could tackle the different styles of exam question
- the format of the exam, including what questions might look like
- how questions might be marked, including examples of answers, with exam comments

How to use this guide

A good way of using this guide is to read it through in the order in which it is presented. Alternatively, you can consider each topic in the Content Guidance section, and then turn to a relevant question in the Questions & Answers section. Whichever way you use the guide, try some of the questions yourself to test your learning.

Glossary

A list of terms is included at the end of this guide (pages 90–94). They are organised alphabetically and subdivided into the two topic areas — biological psychology and learning theories. This is a list of definitions that can help you in your revision. You could also go through the glossary matching terms to topic areas, which will help your learning, picking out all the methodology terms to draw them together.

Questions & Answers

Note that cross-references in the Content Guidance are given to answers in the Questions & Answers section that provide more information on particular areas of content.

Content Guidance

■ Biological psychology

This section looks at biological psychology with its five main parts (content; method; studies; key question; practical investigation). It also has an issues and debates section. In some places in your course you can choose what you study. In this section suitable material is presented, but you may have studied different examples (this is indicated). *You might be better advised to revise the material you chose for your course.*

Content
The central nervous system and neurotransmission, and the effect of recreational drugs on the transmission process. The structure of the brain, brain areas and functioning as an explanation of aggression, and the role of evolution and natural selection to explain aggression. Freud's psychodynamic explanation of aggression (personality, unconscious and catharsis) as an alternative to biological explanations of aggression and the role of hormones, again to explain aggression.
Individual differences and conclusions e.g. from case studies of brain-damaged patients as well as Freud's view highlighting individual differences.
Developmental psychology in considering the role of evolution and the role of hormones.
Methodology
Correlation research including types of correlation, co-variables and the use of scatterdiagrams, as well as issues with correlations such as cause-and-effect and other variables. Analysis of correlations including using Spearman's rho and issues around that related to levels of measurement, critical and observed values, reasons for using the Spearman test and statistical significance. Experiments compared with correlations, including IV and DV, experimental, null and alternate hypotheses, control groups, randomising and sampling. Scanning (PET, fMRI and CAT), one twin and one adoption study — and scanning to investigate human behaviour such as aggression.
Two studies in detail
Raine et al. (1997) and Brendgen et al. (2005) are described and evaluated. You may have studied Li et al. (2013) or van den Oever et al. (2008) instead.
Key question
The issue of how effective drug therapy is for treating addictions is given here, but you may have looked at one or more different key questions.
Practical
You will have carried out at least one practical within biological psychology and you should use your own practical, because you will have 'learned by doing'. Some ideas about the practical are suggested in this book.
Issues and debates*
Unless you are studying at AS, there are 11 issues and debates in your course: ethics; practical issues in the design and implementation of research; reductionism; comparisons of ways of explaining behaviour using different themes; psychology as a science; culture and gender; nature-nurture; understanding of how psychological understanding has developed over time; issues of social control; the use of psychological knowledge in society; issues related to socially sensitive research. **Issues and debates are not required at AS, but they can be useful for evaluation purposes.*

Table 1 Summary of biological psychology in your course

Biological psychology Overview Q1 describes what is meant by biological psychology. What follows is a brief summary.

The biological approach focuses on the brain and related areas to do with our physical functioning, such as hormones. The way we have evolved regarding the brain and behaviour is also focused on. Aggression is used as a behaviour of focus in your course, and the psychodynamic explanation for aggression is used as a contrasting explanation.

The role of the central nervous system and neurotransmitters in human behaviour

The central nervous system (CNS) consists of the brain and spinal cord. The brain guides human behaviour through neurotransmitter functioning.

The central nervous system

The **central nervous system** (CNS) guides our behaviour. It governs incoming messages from the body and also sends messages back from the brain to the body. It coordinates the body's activities.

Neurons and synaptic transmission

The structure of a **neuron** is shown in Figure 1. There is a **cell body** (the nucleus), from which an axon leads, with **myelin sheath** protection, and **nodes of Ranvier** to help the **electrical impulse** (or **action potential**) to travel down the **axon**. The message travels down the axon to axon **terminal buttons**. **Dendrites** come from the nucleus of the cell.

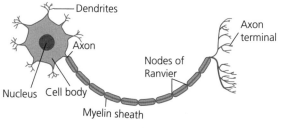

Figure 1 A neuron

Neurotransmitters are stored at the terminal buttons and if the **receptors** at the dendrites of a nearby neuron are a fit for the neurotransmitter, the message carries on from the axon terminal of one neuron, across the gap, and via the dendrites, to the cell body of another neuron. This is **synaptic transmission** (Figure 2). The **synapse** is the gap between the terminal button of one neuron and the dendrite of another.

> **Exam tip**
>
> There could be a question on the central nervous system about the structure and role of the neuron, the function of neurotransmitters and synaptic transmission, or the role of neurotransmitters, so be ready to write about each of these features separately.

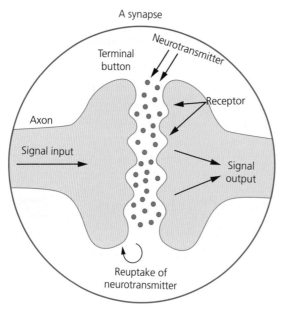

Figure 2 Synaptic transmission

Biological psychology Content Q1 defines four terms relating to neurotransmitter functioning.

Exam tip

A diagram may be used to ask questions — be ready for diagrams that need labelling and/or explaining. You can use a diagram in your own description if it helps, but make sure your labelling is complete and thorough. A diagram on its own is unlikely to earn you full marks as it is not likely to 'describe' fully.

The function of neurotransmitters

There are different neurotransmitters, each with different functions. For example, dopamine is associated with pleasure feelings and seratonin is for happiness and a good mood. Norepinephrine (noradrenaline) is associated with the fight and flight response and with attention, being ready for action. Acetylcholine is linked to memory, thinking and learning.

The function of synaptic transmission

Messages are passed in the brain using synaptic transmission. Neurotransmitters from the terminal buttons of one neuron (the **pre-synaptic neuron**) can be taken up by receptors in the dendrites of another neuron (the **post-synaptic neuron**) and then any spare neurotransmitters can be taken up again to be reused (this is **reuptake**). Without neurotransmitters the message stops so reuptake has an important role —

Exam tip

There are a lot of terms in the explanation of neurons and synaptic transmission. Be ready to define any one of them and to identify them on a diagram. Drawing a mind map of the terms and their definitions, using an order that helps your recall, will reinforce your understanding.

Knowledge check 1

Define the following terms: neuron, synapse, receptor, neurotransmitter and central nervous system.

to stop the message. Reuptake happens in the pre-synaptic neuron. For example, preventing reuptake leaves more of the neurotransmitters there and the message continues (look up Selective Serotonin Reuptake Inhibitors (SSRIs) to see an example of this). There are different receptors in the post-synaptic neuron, related to different neurotransmitters so the messages passed are selective.

Strengths	Weaknesses
Jovanovic (2008) used PET scanning and found differences in the synaptic receptors related to serotonin of women with pre-menstrual dysphoric disorder (PMDD), suggesting a role for serotonin in the disorder — perhaps lack of it being taken up leads to this mood disorder	Allen and Stevens (1994) found that less than half the neurotransmitters in transmission in the hippocampus arrived from the pre-synaptic neuron, being picked up by the post-synaptic neuron. Synaptic transmission is not straightforward
Scanning is a strong method as it can be reliable if more than one person checks the data and the activity measured is 'real' in coming from an individual	Evidence has come from studying lesions (damaged parts of the brain) in animals but generalising from animals to humans might not be a credible thing to do as there are differences

Table 2 Strengths and weaknesses of the synaptic transmission explanation of how messages pass in the brain

Links

Individual differences link

Individual differences are not considered when discussing the process of synaptic transmission by means of neurotransmitters. It is assumed that everyone's brain uses this means of sending messages. However, different people have differences in neurotransmitter functioning, such as a lack (or excess) of a particular neurotransmitter. The processes might be the same, but the messages are affected by individual differences. Someone with low serotonin levels might benefit from medication to increase them, thus alleviating the symptoms of depression, for example.

The effects of recreational drugs on the transmission process in the central nervous system

Recreational drugs are taken for pleasure, which distinguishes them from prescribed drugs like SSRIs. The **mode of action** of a drug is the way it works at the synapse and in the brain.

Mode of action of some recreational drugs

Cocaine

Cocaine acts in the reward centre of the brain. Cocaine blocks the reuptake of dopamine into the pre-synaptic neuron so more dopamine is left in the synapse and the message continues. (If cocaine was not there to block the reuptake, the dopamine would not remain there for as long).

Exam tip

Your answers will be assessed according to the three assessment objectives (page 66). Match your learning about each topic with notes evaluating that topic. Strengths and weaknesses are included here to help you do this. Learn and build on these.

Exam tip

You will need to know about individual differences and where they are considered in biological psychology so make notes about this area of the content. You need to be ready for any questions about this area of psychology.

Knowledge check 2

Why is using brain scanning a better method for finding out about brain processing using synaptic transmission than using studies of animals?

Nicotine

Nicotine works on the reward pathway in the brain to give pleasure. It is addictive because someone will carry out actions to stimulate the reward pathway — there is motivation to do that. Nicotinic receptors trigger an electrical impulse in a neuron and in the reward pathway — the neurotransmitter that will be released is dopamine, giving pleasure.

Cannabis

There are cannabinoid receptors (just as there are dopamine receptors). Cannabis will bind to these receptors to block them. (The receptors accept the cannabis which prevents the neurotransmitter released from the pre-synaptic neuron sending the message in the post-synaptic neuron.) The hippocampus has a lot of cannabinoid receptors and so cannabis can prevent activity in the hippocampus, which is for memory (see cognitive psychology) so cannabis can affect memory. Cannabis can also stop specific neurons from preventing dopamine production in the reward system so there is excess dopamine.

Strengths	Weaknesses
There is a lot of evidence. Olds and Milner (1954) found a pleasure centre in the brain (of rats). Straiker et al. (2012) looked at the effect of cannabis and found an effect in the hippocampus (of mice)	There is a complexity in how transmission works in the brain that is hard to capture (if not impossible given current tools to measure such transmission). Cannabis limits hippocampal activity and leads to more dopamine activity and there is more than one reward pathway
There is credibility in saying that the reward pathway relates to dopamine, which is a neurotransmitter giving pleasure and recreational drugs work on the reward pathway to increase pleasure	Scanning and finding out about receptor activity is not straightforward. Scanning needs to be more sophisticated, for example, and the focus currently is on transmitters that are more easily studied so they are the ones any conclusions will be about

Table 3 Strengths and weaknesses of the arguments about the effects of drugs on transmission

The structure of the brain and human aggression

Four lobes

The brain is made up of four **lobes**: the temporal, parietal, occipital and prefrontal lobes. The hippocampus has already been mentioned when discussing synaptic functioning, and is in the medial temporal lobe (pages 9 and 10). Damage to the prefrontal lobe is linked to aggression. Lobes feature when studying structures of the brain.

Corpus callosum

The **corpus callosum** is important for taking messages between the two halves (hemispheres) of the brain.

Knowledge check 3

With reference to two recreational drugs explain the effect of them on the transmission process in the central nervous system.

Exam tip

It can be hard to remember detail about the mode of action of recreational drugs. Aim to learn how drugs work at the synapse with the relevant neurotransmitters. One way to do this is to draw the synaptic gap (Figure 2) and draw in the way the recreational drug works in a way that you understand.

The prefrontal cortex and aggression

Raine et al. (1997) found that the prefrontal cortex is involved in aggression (pages 26–28). The cortex is the outer layer of the brain. The prefrontal cortex is in the prefrontal lobe and, like other structures in the brain, is found in both hemispheres and has a role in emotions. Depression, for example, links to the orbitofrontal, ventromedial and lateral prefrontal cortices. It is thought that aggression arises because of lack of control from the prefrontal cortex.

Evidence for the prefrontal cortex linking to aggression

- A lot of dopamine, serotonin and norepinephrine connections are found in the prefrontal cortex. These neurotransmitters link to emotions, which is evidence that this area has a role in emotions.
- Bechara and van der Linden (2005) agreed from looking at findings of studies that the prefrontal lobe regulates behaviour and defers rewards, being about planning. Damage to this area (**lesion** is the term used for damage to brain structure) might mean wanting immediate gratification, making someone impatient, so linking to aggression. The prefrontal lobe inhibits messages from the amygdala, which links to it having a planning role and damage there might lead to more negative emotions.
- Raine et al. (1997) found that people who had showed emotional impulsive violence differed in their prefrontal cortex compared with controls (pages 26–28).

The limbic system and aggression

The limbic system includes the hippocampus, amygdala and hypothalamus (Figure 3) and has a role in self-preservation, including response to emotions and the fight-or-flight response, which arouses us when we are in danger. In animals, if the amygdala is stimulated using an electric current there is an aggressive response and if the amydgala is removed the animal is passive.

Knowledge check 4

Explain evidence to show that the prefrontal cortex links to aggression.

Exam tip

You can just say that the prefrontal cortex links with aggression, but giving a named study (e.g. Raine et al., 1997) signals that you know the evidence for the claim. Your exam answers have more weight if you include evidence to support the claims you make.

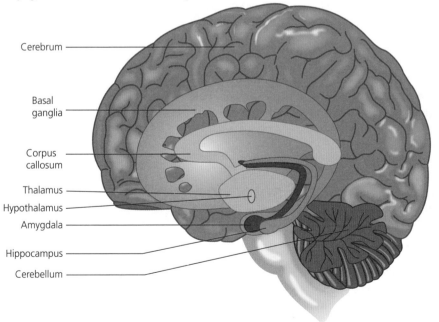

Figure 3 Some structures in the brain

Evidence for the limbic system linking to aggression

- Andy and Velamati (1978) stimulated the hypothalamus and basal ganglia (both in the limbic system) of cats. This led to them having aggressive seizures. They also found that blocking catecholamine increased aggression. Epinephrine, norepinephrine and dopamine are catecholamines. This shows how although brain structure is discussed separately from neurotransmitter functioning the two of course link. Blocking dopamine might lead to worsening of mood, for example (page 8).
- Downer (1961) — monkeys had one amygdala removed (the amygdala goes across the two hemispheres so it is as if there were two). Visual signals go to the amygdala. Visual signals that reached the amygdala led to normal functioning, but when visual signals were sent to the removed amydgala this led to behaviour that was more calm, unlike the cats' normal reactions. (**Ablation** is the term for removing brain structures.)
- Hermans et al. (1993) showed that electrical stimulation of the hypothalamus leads to aggression.

Strengths	Weaknesses
There is a lot of evidence. Human studies (Swantje et al., 2012) show that self-reported aggression links with the size of the amygdala (the smaller the size, the more the aggression). Andy and Velamati (1978) and Downer (1961) provide evidence from animal studies that the amygdala is involved in aggression	Animal studies have been used a lot to investigate the link between aggression and brain functioning, but animals do not have the same prefrontal cortex as humans (it is smaller), as well as having other differences. This makes generalising hard
MRI scanning (Swantje et al., 2012) and PET scanning (Raine et al., 1997) give reliable measurements and can separate brain structures for study. There is scientific credibility in their findings	People do not function normally in brain scanners so there might be a lack of validity in the findings about aggression

Table 4 Strengths and weaknesses of the claim that brain structure relates to aggression

> **Exam tip**
>
> Notice how strengths and weaknesses of evidence for biological factors affecting behaviour include the methods of gathering the evidence, e.g. issues around scanning being reliable but possibly not valid, and animal studies not having generalisable findings (to humans). Remember to think about such general issues when you write about strengths and weaknesses.

The role of evolution and natural selection to explain human behaviour including aggression

Evolution and natural selection

We are a collection of genes, 50% from our mother and 50% from our father — this is our **genotype**. Our **genes** are said to have come from a process of evolution through survival of the fittest genes (those leading to successful behaviour). **Evolution** is how inherited characteristics pass from generation to generation, through reproduction. To survive to reproduce requires certain characteristics that lead to certain

> **Exam tip**
>
> Your course looks at brain structure and functioning as an explanation of aggression as a human behaviour. You can use animal behaviour as evidence, but remember to discuss such evidence in relation to human behaviour (e.g. make the point that findings about animals might not be true of humans).

> **Knowledge check 5**
>
> Give three pieces of evidence that show that brain structure links to aggression.

behaviours and only the genes giving those characteristics will be passed on through reproduction. Some evolution is negative and means the organism will die out as what is inherited through reproduction does not aid survival.

Strengths	Weaknesses
There is a lot of evidence for the theory of natural selection, not only Darwin's evidence (e.g. the differences in finches on different islands), but Kettlewell's evidence too (e.g. the colour of moths suits their environment), and much more	By reducing behaviour that is observed (e.g. to behaviour that would be inherited) the whole of behaviour of an organism is not studied. This can miss out important elements of complex activity that organisms, including humans, display
The evidence is gathered using scientific methods, including reducing behaviour to something observable and gathering evidence carefully so that cause-and-effect conclusions can be made	Many believe in creationism of some sort, which is where God created earth and humans. There are different explanations for how this might have happened, but all have the same underlying belief. The theory of natural selection goes against creationist beliefs

Table 5 Strengths and weaknesses of natural selection as an explanation for human behaviour

Evolution, natural selection and aggression

Not only would behaviours that come from genes survive, such as birds having suitable beak shapes to find food in different habitats, but emotions would survive too. It has been shown that aggression, for example, links to various human brain structures like the amygdala. It could be that humans with an aggressive rather than a passive response to danger survived and so the amygdala as it is in humans today is one that helped survival. Living peacefully in groups might help survival so we might have inherited that tendency. Aggression in response to an attack on offspring might have led to survival of the offspring and so the aggressive response survived (or the brain structure and functioning that supported that response survived).

Links

Developmental psychology link

Survival of the fittest, leading to genetic features in us, clearly affects our development. Our genotype has evolved as particular useful genes and gene combinations have been passed on through reproduction. Others died out as our ancestors with those combinations and genes did not survive to reproduce.

Questions & Answers

Biological psychology Content Q3 discusses how biological psychology helps us to understand how people develop, using the idea of survival of the fittest and inherited characteristics.

Exam tip

In biological psychology you look at brain structure and functioning to explain aggression in humans. You consider the idea of evolution to explain human behaviour *including* aggression. You also consider the role of hormones to explain human behaviour *such as* aggression. Note the differences in what is required.

Evidence for survival of the fittest theory linking to aggression

- Buss and Shackleton (1997) found men tend to give in to 'their' female and were threatening to other males around — both strategies being useful for the survival of their genes.
- Lorenz (1966) held that aggression has evolved, in that it helps, in males in particular, fighting over limited resources.

Strengths	Weaknesses
There is a lot of evidence for the theory of natural selection including Buss and Shackleton (1997) and Lorenz (1966), as well as Darwin's evidence. As an explanation of aggression, protecting offspring and mates, it has strong evidence	The theory requires other theories such as kin selection to help to explain how behaviours that draw attention to an individual so they might not survive to reproduce their genes still remain as behaviours today. Kin selection is the idea that organisms can draw attention to themselves so their genes do not seem to continue but in doing so they protect their kin, so the genes do in fact continue
The theory comes from scientific study and has scientific credibility, including being widely accepted in the scientific community. It explains aggression in terms of protection of the individual's genes by protecting mate and offspring as well as protecting self — a widely accepted idea	An opposing theory is the frustration-aggression hypothesis, which can explain aggression that does not link to protecting mate and offspring or self. The frustration-aggression hypothesis can explain aggression against strangers, for example, in a more complete way

Table 6 Strengths and weaknesses of the evolution explanation for human aggression

The role of hormones to explain human behaviour such as aggression

Like neurotransmitters, **hormones** carry messages. Although both involve chemicals, hormones carry messages more slowly, travelling in the blood stream, whereas neurotransmitters are in neurons. Hormones are produced by endocrine glands, which are groups of cells. They affect growth and other processes such as metabolism, which is the way the body converts food into energy, and they affect mood. They also have a role in growth and development. Examples include hormones produced in the pituitary gland which help body regulation and the pineal gland which produces melatonin, which links to sleep.

Links

Developmental psychology link

Hormones affect our development. For example, it is the androgens in the foetus which lead to the development of a male child and testosterone is an androgen. The foetus without the effects of male hormones is female. Hormones also affect growth and metabolism, as well as sleep — all factors that can affect our development.

Knowledge check 6

Explain the theory of natural selection using the example of aggression.

Exam tip

When evaluating a theory it is useful to give as a weakness the idea of another theory that either explains the situation just as well or better. You can evaluate the other theory perhaps just once, to add to the argument, but make sure your answer does not turn into one about the other theory.

Hormones work by changing cell function. They bind to receptor proteins in cells. Changes in the environment (like changes in light) can trigger the release of hormones. Not only is behaviour changed by the arrival of hormones at the receptors, but also by how concentrated they are (their levels).

Evidence for the effects of hormones related to aggression

Dabbs et al. (1987) measured testosterone (a male hormone) in the saliva of 89 male prisoners, some involved in violent crime and some in non-violent crime. They found 10 of the 11 prisoners involved in violent crime had high levels of testosterone compared with a 9 in 11 chance of those with low testosterone levels being involved in non-violent crime. Also those with high testosterone levels were rated by their peers as 'tough'.

Barzman et al. (2013) look at hormones in the saliva of 7 to 9 year old boys in a psychiatric hospital. They took saliva samples from 17 boys and looked for DHEA (a hormone), testosterone and cortisol. They also obtained ratings of the aggression of the children (e.g. from the nurses). They found that the amount of cortisol in the saliva just after waking correlated with the number of aggressive incidents recorded by the nurse. There were other findings too. It was thought that using saliva to measure hormones was a useful method.

Chang et al. (2012) used fish to look at hormones and aggression. They found that aggression, exploring behaviour and 'boldness' in the fish correlated with the amount of testosterone before the behaviours. Aggression and boldness also correlated with the amount of cortisol before the behaviours.

Strengths	Weaknesses
Studies tend to use a lot of controls, even if they find correlational data and not differences. Barzman et al. (2013) used standardised measures for the children to rate their aggression and tests of hormones found in saliva to measure the hormone levels. These are carefully controlled measures	Studies using humans tend to show correlations between levels of testosterone and cortisol and aggression, and correlations do not give cause-and-effect findings. This is not as scientific as gathering evidence from which cause-and-effect conclusions can be drawn. Another variable, not in the study, might relate to both the aggression and the hormones
Both human and animal studies have found a link between cortisol and testosterone and aggression. There are so many studies, using different methods and measures, that have found this link that this gives scientific credibility and reliability to the findings	If aggression links to hormones such as testosterone and cortisol, and also to low levels of the neurotransmitter serotonin — and also to certain aggression centres in the brain — then reducing biological explanations to hormones, neurotransmitter functioning or brain structure, is not going to give a holistic explanation for human aggression

Table 7 Strengths and weaknesses of the hormone explanation for human aggression

Knowledge check 7

Using evidence from human studies, give evidence to show that hormones might link to aggressive behaviour.

Exam tip

Biological theories include the role of neurotransmitters, survival of the fittest and the passing on of genes, and the role of hormones. Draw a diagram/mindmap with 'Biological explanations of human aggression' in the centre and add the explanations around that, including detail and evaluation points. This will help you to see the overall picture.

The psychodynamic explanation for aggression

As a contrast to standard biological explanations for aggression, the psychodynamic approach is worth studying and is in your course for that purpose.

Id, ego and superego: the personality

Links

Individual differences link

In Freud's theory the id, ego and superego develop in each individual, giving their individual differences.

The **id** according to Freud and his psychodynamic theory is the main part of our personality. It is the 'I want' part, is there at birth, and is not accessible to us, being unconscious. The **superego** develops later, when we are about 3 years old or older. The superego is the conscience and the ego ideal. This means it consists of all that we are told not to do, and is about us becoming socialised. It also gives us the 'ego ideal' — the person we should be. The **ego** is the reasoning part of the personality, balancing the hidden desires of the id with the demands of the superego as to what we should be.

Links

Developmental psychology link

In Freud's theory the id, ego and superego develop in each individual, giving their individual differences, which is about how we develop from birth. He also put forward the idea of developmental stages, which he called 'psychosocial stages' within which the id, ego and superego develop.

Unconscious, preconscious, conscious

Freud thought the mind was made up of three parts. The **conscious** mind is what we are aware of. The **preconscious** mind has thoughts and ideas we can access but they are not conscious at the time. The **unconscious** mind is the main/largest part. It is where all thoughts come from, some becoming conscious, some in the preconscious — many not known and not knowable though, remain in the unconscious. The unconscious is not passive — we use energy keeping thoughts, wishes and ideas unconscious.

Questions & Answers

Biological psychology Content Q2 explains the role of the unconscious.

Exam tip

There are biological elements to the psychodynamic theory, but it is officially 'non-biological'. Be sure when you are writing about this theory you make it clear that this is the case. If asked for a biological theory of aggression, do not use the psychodynamic theory in your answer.

Freud's theory and aggression: catharsis

Freud put forward the idea of us having drives. One drive is the sex drive, the libido — the drive for self-preservation. Another drive is **thanatos**, the so-called death drive, which is about an individual wanting to go back to the state of 'not being'. Another drive is **eros**, the 'life instinct'. In order to preserve the self and respond to our drives, our ego works to balance the demands of the id against the restrictions of the superego. The ego does this by repressing unacceptable thoughts into the unconscious. Once such desires are made conscious he believed we would be free of them. They would no longer take up energy and hold us back. **Defence mechanisms** can help to keep unwelcome thoughts unconscious, such as denying the issue (**denial**) or using displacement to push the thoughts onto someone 'safer' — not the real target of them.

In this approach aggression helps to preserve life, as the death instinct is subdued by it. Freud felt that it was frustration (such as not being able to avoid pain or not being able to get pleasure) that led to aggression. The superego is the child's conscience and the child is frustrated by being stopped from doing something it wants, and aggression can be the result. Love for the parents stops the child from actually being aggressive. The child may have a very strong conscience and superego to sublimate the aggression. The aggression, however, is not released which can be problematic.

If aggressive and frustrated thoughts can be brought into the conscious mind, the release is what Freud called **catharsis**. The energy taken up to keep such thoughts and aggression unconscious is released and can be used elsewhere.

Evidence for catharsis

- Hokanson (1974, in Verona and Sullivan, 2008) found that behaving in an aggressive way reduced tension in the individual as shown by biological measures, which is evidence for catharsis.
- Verona and Sullivan (2008) found in their own study that people who reacted in an aggressive way to being made frustrated in a task had a reduced heart rate compared with those who did not react aggressively, giving evidence for aggression being cathartic.

Evidence against catharsis

- However, Hokanson (1974, in Verona and Sullivan, 2008) found that reduction in tension after behaving aggressively seemed to increase the likelihood of later aggression, which goes against the idea of catharsis — at least it suggests it does not last long.
- Bushman et al. (1999, in Verona and Sullivan, 2008) found that those who read an article saying that hitting a punch bag was cathartic, were more likely to hit out at a punch bag after having negative feedback about an essay they wrote, than those who did not read about catharsis. It seems that reading about it did not release the aggression, in fact it led to more aggression.

Exam tip

Freud's psychodynamic theory uses a lot of terms. If you can define the terms you can probably put together a good answer about the theory. Use definitions of id, ego, superego, conscious, preconscious, unconscious, catharsis, thanatos and eros to write the 'story' of his theory. Add evaluation points too.

Strengths	Weaknesses
Freud's theory has led to a lot of different 'talking' therapies that focus on, if not unconscious desires, thoughts and desires that are not easily accessed. Such as cognitive behavioural therapy which aims to uncover core beliefs and person-centred therapy which aims to highlight conditionality in our thinking ('if we do X, then we are bad...') that comes from learning from others	There is evidence for his theory (e.g. Verona and Sullivan, 2008), but there is also evidence against it. Bandura's studies (pages 40–43 in learning theories) suggest that aggression is learned from watching others and far from this being cathartic it actually leads to aggression
Freud used in-depth **case studies** of individuals and his theory came from the stories of his patients. The data were valid and his analysis was in depth	Findings from case studies of individuals are hard to generalise to everyone and to draw a universal theory from

Table 8 Strengths and weaknesses of Freud's explanation for human aggression

Questions & Answers

Biological psychology Content Q2 discusses how the psychodynamic approach might be unscientific, which can help with its evaluation.

Exam tip

You can be asked to describe something (e.g. a theory). You can also be asked to explain. 'Explain' means give a point and then justify it. You can find out about such command words by looking at Appendix 6 in your specification — the taxonomy.

Knowledge check 8

Define what is meant by 'credibility' when applied to psychological findings and give two criticisms of Freud's work with regard to its credibility.

Individual differences

In the content sections for biological psychology the importance of individual differences has been noted. Here is a summary:

- Neurotransmitter functioning is the same for everyone in how it works, but the specifics of neurotransmitter functioning can be affected by individual differences.
- Freud's theory of personality, where the id, ego and superego work together regarding decision making for each individual, reflects individual differences.

Developmental psychology

In the content sections for biological psychology the importance of issues for our development has been noted. Here is a summary:

- Survival of the fittest is a theory of development.
- Hormones affect our development.
- Freud's theory discusses how we develop through the ego making decisions to balance the superego and id.

Summary

- Biological psychology looks at the central nervous system (the brain and spinal cord) and how neurotransmitters send messages in the brain. This includes the function and structure of a neuron, through studying synaptic functioning, which involves neurotransmitters.
- Recreational drugs work in the brain at the synapses and the effect of recreational drugs on the transmission process in the central nervous system is covered.
- The structure of the brain, including looking at brain areas that help to explain aggression, is a focus of study, looking at brain functioning. Such areas include the prefrontal cortex and the amygdala.
- As an alternative to biological ways of explaining aggression, and not part of biological psychology, Freud's pyschodynamic explanation of aggression is considered. This means looking at his idea about personality — the id, ego and superego and the way they work together, as well as looking at the role of the unconscious and the idea of catharsis. The general idea is that aggression is a drive that can be released from the unconscious by being aggressive and that is helpful for an individual.
- A final explanation for human behaviour like aggression is hormones. These, like neurotransmitters, send messages around the body including the brain, though they take messages more slowly and via the blood stream. Hormones that relate to aggression include testosterone and cortisol.
- Alongside the main content you need to learn about, you need to make notes about where individual differences are covered in biological psychology — Freud's personality theory is about individual differences as can be specific brain damage, leading to specific difficulties for individuals.
- Developmental psychology also needs to be noted, such as Freud's theory about how we develop. Hormones also have a role in our development.

Method

Correlational research

One way of gathering correlational data is to use self-report data, which are obtained when participants judge themselves on a particular category. Any scale where the participant has to rate something is a rating scale, for example judging someone's attractiveness on a scale of 1 to 5.

In studies with a correlational design, there are two scores, a score for each of two **co-variables**. For example, two scores could be age and the number of words that can be recalled from a list. So for each participant, both these scores are found. Perhaps the older someone is, the fewer items they can recall, and this would be a correlation. In this example age and items recalled would be co-variables — they vary together.

- **Negative correlations** are when one score rises as the other falls. An example would be: the higher the age, the lower the number of items recalled from a list.
- **Positive correlations** are when as one score rises, the other rises as well. An example would be: the higher the happiness rating of someone, the longer the relationship.

Correlations are about maths and statistics and are presented in that way. A perfect positive correlation is +1 and a perfect negative correlation is −1, with 0

Knowledge check 9

Note down for the following correlation scores whether you think they would be significant if a test were to be done, and what else you can say about them. The scores are +0.62 and −0.57.

being no correlation at all. A perfect positive correlation would be when in every case as one score rises the other rises too; and a perfect negative correlation would be when in every case as one score rises, the other falls. Note that a negative correlation *is* a correlation. It is 0 that means no correlation at all — when there is no relationship. If the result of testing for a correlation is near +1 or –1 (e.g. 0.78) it is a fairly **strong correlation**. The nearer it is to 0 (e.g. 0.20) the weaker the correlation.

Strengths	Weaknesses
Good for finding relationships at the start of an investigation; also unexpected relationships; once two sets of data are collected from the same participants, a test can be carried out to see if there is a correlation between them	Only suggests a relationship; this does not mean that the two variables are causally related; they may only show a relationship by chance or because of some other factor. Some other variable might be causing the apparent link
There are no participant variables as the same participant gives both scores	Data may not be valid because the measures may be artificial or unconnected

Table 9 Strengths and weaknesses of correlation as a research design

Analysis of correlational data

To analyse correlations, you need first to list both sets of scores and then rank each set of scores separately. After that, study the rankings — and look to see if high ranks go together and low ranks go together, or if high ranks go consistently with low ranks and vice versa.

Ranking data involves starting from the lowest score and giving that rank 1 and continuing (some books say start with the highest and give that 1, the same result will be found). The only difficulty is if some scores are the same, in which case you give those scores the same rank, but in a way that keeps an equivalent number of ranks. So if there are three scores of 8 and they follow rank 3, you share out ranks 4, 5 and 6 between the three '8' scores, giving each a rank of 5. Then you carry on from rank 7. This is the same as finding the median of the scores because to find the median you have to rank the scores first.

Scores	1	3	5	8	8	8	9	14	20
Rank	1	2	3	5	5	5	7	8	9

Table 10 How to rank scores

You can also draw a **scatter diagram** of the scores and look at the line of best fit to see whether there is a correlation or not. The graph in Figure 4 uses a made-up set of scores, illustrating a positive correlation, and you can see how as one score rises, the other rises too.

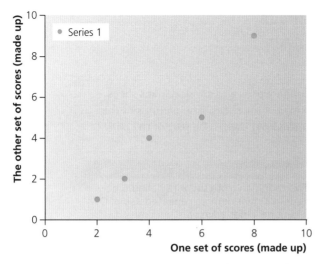

Figure 4 Scatter diagram to show positive correlation

Exam tip

You need to be able to sense check set(s) of data, not only using rankings and scatter diagrams, but any set of scores, to look to see if there might be significance before doing one of the inferential tests. Practise doing this.

Knowledge check 10

Show what is meant by each of the following terms through the use of an example: positive correlation, negative correlation, self-report data, ranking and sense checking data.

When you analyse a correlation, the scatter diagram and a look at the rankings should tell you whether you are expecting there to be a relationship or not and whether it is likely to be a positive or a negative correlation. You can **sense check** the data before doing a statistical test. It is useful to have an idea about the result beforehand.

You can also use statistical testing (e.g. the Spearman Rank Correlation Coefficient) to see if there is a correlation. How to use statistical tests was explained in *Edexcel Psychology: Social psychology and cognitive psychology (with issues and debates) Student Guide* (page 49). There are also important terms to know about, which are covered in learning theories in this book (pages 53–55).

Experiments versus correlations

- Experiments have experimental **hypotheses**. Correlations have alternate hypotheses (as they are not experiments). Both have a null hypothesis to test against.
- Experiments have an **independent** and a **dependent variable** (IV and DV) whereas correlations have co-variables. A correlation can have an IV and a DV if the researcher makes the decision about which they are interested in. If they are interested more in temperature than in aggression, temperature is the IV.
- Correlations get data from the same person or from general figures (e.g. daily temperature), not from individual participants in different conditions. Experiments have **control groups** and **randomise** when allocating people to groups.
- Both correlations and experiments use **sampling**, though it is in experiments that sampling is important because of the use of groups. In social psychology in your course you learned about four types of sampling — random, stratified, opportunity and volunteer sampling. Remind yourself about those for this topic area.

Other biological research methods

Brain scanning techniques: CAT, PET, fMRI

CAT/CT scanning

X-ray computed tomography (CAT or CT) scanning uses an x-ray and takes slices of sections of the brain/body producing drawings of the slices. The pictures of the slices can be put together to form a three-dimensional image of a part of the body or area of interest.

Strengths	Weaknesses
It gives detail that was not there before scanning — such as not being affected by overlap of organs in the body, and being able to produce three-dimensional imaging, including from different angles. So for evidence of damage to the brain, it is very useful	The radiation from the x-ray should be kept to a minimum so repeated use of CT scanning is not advised. This limits its effectiveness and also is an ethical issue
Non-invasive and painless, which is a strength for the individual though using a dye like iodine is invasive to an extent. It is not as invasive as surgery, so the strength remains	MRI scanning can be better for certain issues. For example, seeing what is causing headaches is better using an MRI scan, but looking for skull fractures is better using a CT scan.

Table 11 Strengths and weaknesses of CT scanning

PET scanning

Positron emission tomography (PET) scanning picks up 'hot' areas in the brain to see which part of the brain is working in specific circumstances. A radioactive tracer is added to glucose (or another chemical that the body uses) and is injected into the arm. The tracer gives small, positively charged particles called positrons, which give out signals that can be displayed as images for interpretation.

A PET scan studies blood flow in the brain to show which areas are active (e.g. when talking) and can also show the size of brain areas so they can be measured and compared between people (see Raine et al., 1997, pages 26–28). The radioactive tracer does not last long.

Strengths	Weaknesses
PET scans are valid because their findings match other findings and they do measure what they claim to measure (e.g. the area pinpointed for speech is the same as that found by other methods)	They are ethical up to a point because they are relatively non-invasive compared with surgery; but, the injection is invasive. They can be distressing
PET scans are reliable; they are replicable and the same areas are highlighted (e.g. Broca's area for speech)	It is hard to pinpoint exact areas of the brain so even if PET scans are clear, they are still fairly broad in their imaging

Table 12 Strengths and weaknesses of PET scanning

fMRI scanning

Functional magnetic resonance imaging (fMRI) picks up on changes of use of brain areas depending on the task being carried out. Blood flow and neuronal activity are linked so changes in blood flow relate to neuronal activity. The fMRI looks at the

Exam tip

Use your textbook or some other source to find examples of studies that have used fMRI, CAT/CT and PET scanning that you can use in your exam. Raine et al. (1997), your classic study, used PET scanning, for example. Try to find examples linked to human aggression too.

blood flow showing brain cell use of energy. It can look at differences in blood flow to a high degree of accuracy and is useful for issues like being at risk of stroke.

Strengths	Weaknesses
fMRI scans are safer than other scans such as the PET scan, as there is no invasion, surgery or radiation	The fMRI cannot measure the brain at rest (the brain is never at rest, so this applies to PET too) and so there is no baseline measure and it is hard to pinpoint actual functioning for a specific activity. The brain is always active in more than one area
They are very precise in their data and with the brain being so complex, precision is required when it comes to finding out about brain structure and brain functioning	fMRI cannot look at the actual receptors of neurotransmitters whereas PET scanning can do that, so fMRI does not fully replace PET scanning

Table 13 Strengths and weaknesses of fMRI scanning

The use of brain scanning techniques to investigate human behaviour such as aggression

In your course the area to focus on with regard to using brain scanning is aggression.

- Raine et al. (1997) used PET scanning to measure the size of brain areas to see if murderers had differences in the areas known to link to aggression. This was to gather evidence that their aggression had come from brain issues.
- Betts (2009) suggested that a case where a man strangled his wife (aggressive behaviour) could have been due to brain damage and CAT scanning was used to gather the evidence.
- Matthies et al. (2012) used MRI scanning and showed that the size of the amygdala related to the life-time aggression score, showing links between brain structure and aggression.
- Reimann and Zimbardy (2011) carried out a meta-analysis and found, using neuroimaging (scanning), areas in the brain related to aggressive behaviour including the amygdala and the prefrontal cortex.

Strengths	Weaknesses
Meta-analyses use the findings of many studies and compare them. If they agree (which they do) then that gives reliability to the conclusions	There is no baseline level as the brain is always active and other thoughts or processing are likely. Therefore, drawing conclusions with a baseline to give normal functioning is not easy
There seems to be some validity in brain scanning, and it does seem to measure brain functioning, but the relating to actual behaviour might not be so valid	The person has to be 'made aggressive' in some studies, to see what effect that has on brain functioning, and that might not be a valid behaviour or state of mind

Table 14 Strengths and weaknesses of using scanning to find out about human behaviour like aggression

Twin study

One twin study is Brendgen et al. (2005) which is explained as the contemporary study (pages 28–29). Brendgen et al. (2005) helps to explain why **twin studies** are useful. MZ twins share 100% of their genes while DZ twins share just 50%. If MZ twins

Exam tip

Be ready to use evidence from studies in your answers. Use names in your revision so that you get used to using them.

Knowledge check 11

For each of the three scanning techniques you need for your course, give one weakness.

share a characteristic more than DZ twins then that characteristic is likely to have at least an element of genetics. When looking at MZ versus DZ twins the **concordance rate** is how far when one twin has the characteristic the other one has it too. MZ refers to **monozygotic twins**, which share one egg and are identical (including gender). DZ refers to **dizygotic twins**, which have one egg each and are non-identical (can be of different gender).

Issues include:

- MZ twins do not share exactly the same environment, even in the womb, so they develop differently.
- MZ twins have small physical differences such as fingerprints.
- There is **epigenetic modification** which means different environments will cause different genes to be switched on and off. Young MZ twins have few epigenetic differences, older ones show differences as environment is different and more so perhaps over time.

For the usefulness of using twin studies see Brendgen et al. (2005) (pages 28–29).

Strengths	Weaknesses
There is no other way to study genetic influences so clearly because only MZ twins have 100% of their DNA in common	MZ twins have identical DNA, but epigenetic modification has to be taken into account and they may grow and develop differently because of environmental influences
MZ twins and DZ twins share their environments, so there is a natural control over environmental effects	MZ twins may be treated more alike than DZ twins because they are the same sex and look identical; so their environments may not be as controlled as might be thought

Table 15 Strengths and weaknesses of using twin studies to understand human behaviour

Questions & Answers

Biological psychology Method Q1 gives an answer on evaluating twin studies as a research method.

Exam tip

You need to know one twin study and one adoption study, rather than the methods. However, be sure you know about such methods in general as you can be asked to use your twin or adoption study to draw from it information about the methods used and, for example, how they relate to the **nature–nurture debate**.

Adoption study

Adoption studies are similar to twin studies in that they can help to separate genes (nature) from environment (nurture) when studying human behaviour and characteristics. An adopted child has the environment of their adoptive family and the genes of their biological parents. If they show behaviour or characteristics that are similar to their biological parents (who they are not brought up with), then that would suggest genes 'cause' that behaviour rather than environment and nurture.

Strengths	Weaknesses
They control for environment because the children do not share the environment with their biological parent; therefore, similarities with biological parents are genetic. This is hard to do any other way	Families that adopt are similar to each other, so there may be something in that similarity that is causing the results
Studies can be longitudinal, so developmental trends can be studied	Families that adopt tend to be chosen to be as similar as possible to the biological families, so the environment may not be very different

Table 16 Strengths and weaknesses of using adoption studies to understand human behaviour

Leve et al. (2010): an adoption study

One adoption study is briefly outlined here. You may have studied a different adoption study and might prefer to revise that one instead.

Leve et al. (2010) worked on the Early Growth and Development Study (EGDS) in the USA. Its aim was to look at the interaction between an adopted child's genes and their adoptive environment with a view to seeing what interventions might be put in place to help the child and families.

There was a lot of careful work in their study to check that the sample had no bias. This was important so that findings about genes and environment could be generalisable to all adoption situations in the USA.

The EGDS study used many different methods: face-to-face interviews; questionnaires; observation; samples of saliva for cortisol testing; and other testing. They collected data at many times from when the adopted child was 6 months through to 7 years old.

Results reported in this particular part of the EGDS study showed that children who tended to keep their attention on a frustrating task (which another study showed went with them showing aggressive behaviour when they were older) were affected by an adoptive mother's anxiety or depression, whereas if an adoptive mother was not anxious or depressed this characteristic was less evident. This result led to the conclusion that genetic issues in an adopted child interacted with environmental issues. The researchers felt that findings like this could be used to inform interventions to help such children and the adoptive families.

Exam tip

In Knowledge check 12 the wording is 'adoption studies as a method' and 'twin studies as a method'. If the wording was 'compare adoption studies with twin studies' you would not know whether to look at actual studies or at the method used. Questions should be clear — be sure to read them carefully.

Knowledge check 12

Compare adoption studies as a method with twin studies as a method. Make two comparison points.

Strengths	Weaknesses
Leve et al. (2010) used correlational analysis to check that the demographics of the different parts of the sample were not sufficiently different demographically for generalisability to be a problem	They claimed a link between issues like keeping focus on a frustrating issue and later aggressive behaviour, and had evidence from another study to back them, but there are many variables in their study and inferences have to be made
The researchers gathered data using a lot of different methods which meant they could use triangulation to check the reliability of data	Inferring genetic influence from looking at birth mother and child similarities is not the same as using DNA to show genotype. The results reported in this study were limited in the way they drew conclusions about the adopted child's genetic profile

Table 17 Strengths and weaknesses of Leve et al. (2010)

Summary

- Correlations can be negative, where one variable rises the other falls, in a pattern. They can be positive, where one variable rises and the other rises too, in a pattern.
- Correlations can be strong (close to a perfect positive correlation, which is +1 or close to a perfect negative correlation, which is −1) or weak (nearer 0).
- Correlations tend to use co-variables, in that two variables are said to vary together (they co-vary). However, they can have an IV and a DV if one is chosen by the researcher (e.g. the researcher can want to study the effect of age on reaction time so the IV is age and reaction time is the DV).
- Correlations show a pattern between two variables — they do not show a cause-and-effect relationship. There are other variables that might cause the relationship, not the two that are being analysed.
- The pattern can be seen using a scatter diagram which is one way of analysing the data.

- Spearman's rho is the test for correlations that can have ordinal or interval/ratio data. Levels of measurement, critical and observed values, reasons for choosing a statistical test, and issues of statistical significance, as well as inferential statistical testing (using the Spearman's rho) are summarised in learning theories (pages 53–56). They were covered in more detail in *Edexcel Psychology: Social psychology and cognitive psychology (with issues and debates) Student Guide* (page 49).
- Experiments have control groups and use randomising to groups — issues that are not there in correlations, where two scores are compared purely to see if there is a relationship not to see if one causes the other.
- Brain scanning is a method used in biological psychology to investigate human behaviour such as aggression — PET, CAT/CT, fMRI.
- You need one twin study and one adoption study to illustrate these two research methods.

Studies

Classic study: Raine et al. (1997)

Raine et al. (1997) wanted to see if there were brain differences between murderers pleading not guilty by reason of insanity and non-murderers.

- In the study there were 41 murderers (or people charged with manslaughter, but called murderers in this study) pleading insanity and 41 non-murderers in a control group.
- The control group was matched with regard to various features, to make sure the data were comparable.

- The study took place at the University of California and PET scans were done to gather evidence for the 'insanity' plea or some other part of their trial.
- This is an independent groups but matched design.
- The IV is whether a participant is a 'murderer' or not.
- The DV is the various measures of brain activity and brain structure found using PET scanning.

Each participant carried out a practice test. Then they were injected with a trace, after which they completed some more tasks such as recognising a target. After about half an hour of uptake of the trace a PET scan was carried out and images of slices of the brain were produced.

Slices were checked for glucose levels. Boxes of the brain rather than slices were also examined and linked scan results to the suggested areas for violence. The glucose levels and the brain pictures of the murderers were compared with those of the controls.

Results

The tasks that the participants did before the scans were compared to make sure there were no differences in ability and so on, and there were none. Some of the results for the study are given here:

- The murderers had lower glucose metabolism in some prefrontal areas (the front of the brain).
- The murderers had lower glucose metabolism in the corpus callosum (the structure that joins the two halves of the brain).
- The murderers had different levels of activity in the amygdala (an area of the brain linked to aggression).

There were other features of the groups that might have affected results. Use your textbook to remind yourself more about the results.

Questions & Answers

Biological psychology Studies Q1 gives two of Raine et al.'s results.

Conclusions

It was concluded that the murderers had lower glucose activity levels in some brain areas, such as the corpus callosum. They also had abnormal activity in the amygdala and other areas. This suggests that violence has a biological cause. For example, prefrontal deficits can mean loss of self-control, and murderers had different levels of activity in the prefrontal region of the brain. However, the researchers did not conclude that there were only biological causes for violence, just that there might be a predisposition to violence in some people, depending on environmental triggers.

Knowledge check 13

What would you say to someone who said murderers and those charged with murder cannot help such behaviour as it comes from brain differences, which they cannot control?

Exam tip

Bullet points are used here to summarise the study. However, in your exam answer you should avoid bullet points because you are likely then to use shorthand rather than explaining your points fully.

Exam tip

For the methodology part of the biological approach, you need to be able to describe the method of PET scanning. You can use the Raine et al. study to illustrate your description.

Strengths	Weaknesses
PET scanning is an objective technique and the results can be interpreted by more than one researcher; it is a scientific method and is likely to give reliable findings	Hard to generalise beyond murderers pleading not guilty by reason of insanity as there were no violent criminals in the control group
Largest sample size (up to 1997) for PET scanning and large enough for useful comparison with the control group and for generalisation to murderers pleading not guilty by reason of insanity	Does not show biological causes for violence because the environment can cause brain differences

Table 18 Strengths and weaknesses of Raine et al. (1997)

Contemporary study: Brendgen et al. (2005)

You have three contemporary studies to choose from. They are Li et al. (2013), Brendgen et al. (2005) and van den Oever et al. (2008). Brendgen et al. (2005) is summarised here, but if you have studied one of the other two you might prefer to revise your own chosen study. Your textbook will give your more detail.

Brendgen et al. (2005) used 234 six-year-old twins (both non identical of the same sex and identical, the same sex) to look at social and physical aggression to see if these two types of aggression correlate. The researchers also tried to see if such aggression comes from the environment or genes. They used twins with a shared environment and twins with a non-shared environment to find this out. They used **secondary data** in that they did not collect the data directly themselves but used an ongoing twin study which was already gathering relevant data.

Teachers and peers rated the twins for both social and physical aggression — methods that show good reliability and validity for measuring children.

The usefulness of using twin studies

MZ twins share 100% of their genes and DZ twins share just 50% of their genes. And yet they tend to share an environment with one another. The usefulness of twin studies is that comparing MZ twins and DZ twins can show genetic contribution in a way that is otherwise hard to do.

Results

- There was a moderate link in that those showing social aggression also showed physical aggression.
- There were very few gender differences in the findings.
- Brendgen et al. (2005) found that MZ correlations for physical aggression (teacher and peer ratings) were nearly twice as high as for same-sex DZ twins. This suggests a strong genetic contribution to physical aggression.
- MZ and DZ twins were more similar in the correlation for social aggression, which suggests that as both share their environment with one another, social aggression might come from the shared environment.
- With regard to physical aggression and the teacher ratings they thought about 63% was due to genes, and 37% due to a non-shared environment. With regard to physical aggression and the peer ratings they thought about 54% was due to genes, and 46% due to a non-shared environment. In both, there was no effect from a shared environment.

- Social aggression was more evenly split between genetic, shared and non-shared environment, but for both the teacher and peer ratings a large percentage was down to a non-shared environment.

Conclusions

There were many conclusions but an important one was that environmental influences are stronger in social aggression than in physical aggression.

Strengths	Weaknesses
There are two types of ratings, asking similar questions about the same people so reliability can be tested for. In fact the two types of ratings often did agree	Ratings may not match 'reality' — as there is no actual observation, social and physical aggression must be recalled. This might not be a valid way of measuring the two types of aggression
Twin studies, comparing MZ and DZ twins, is a standard way to look for genetic and environmental factors relating to a behaviour, also in this study just same-sex DZ twins were used, which is a control. The method has scientific **credibility**	The non-shared environment might not be as 'non-shared' as it might seem as twins might share the same friends at school, depending perhaps on whether they are in the same class or whether it is a large school

Table 19 Strengths and weaknesses of Brendgen et al. (2005)

Summary

- For biological psychology, as with other topic areas in your course, you need to cover one classic study and one contemporary study from a choice of three.
- The classic study in biological psychology is Raine et al. (1997) who used PET scanning with people who were pleading not guilty to murder by reason of insanity compared with PET scans of a control group. The aim was to look for brain differences between the two groups.

- For the contemporary study in learning theories you can choose Li et al. (2013) who studied brain functioning in heroin-addicted users.
- Or you can choose to study Brendgen et al. (2005) who studied social and physical aggression in identical and non-identical twins to look for genetic factors in aggression.
- Or you can choose to study van den Oever et al. (2008) who studied rats to look at brain changes in response to cues related to heroin addiction.

Key question

You need to know about one key question which biological psychology concepts and research can explain. The question must be important to today's society. One key question is looked at in this book. However, you may have studied another one and might prefer to revise that one.

How effective is drug therapy for treating addiction?

Describing the question

- The number of opiate users in England in 2013/2014 was 293,879 and the number of adults successfully using drug therapy to become free of drugs was 29,150 (according to Public Health England). The high figures here show it is an issue for society, both in terms of cost for the individual and cost to society.

- Addiction relates to cravings and compulsion to take the drug, and some national bodies, such as the National Institutes of Health in the USA, see addiction as a brain disease that needs treating.
- Treatment has to cover all aspects of someone's life because cues can lead to relapse. Substitute drugs are one means of treatment, called 'substitute prescribing' and drugs might be methodone or buprenorphine. What is good is that withdrawal symptoms are then better controlled than if drug therapy was not prescribed.

Concepts, theories and research from biological psychology in your course

Explaining the effectiveness of drug therapy for addiction using theories, concepts and studies from biological psychology

Questions & Answers

Biological psychology Key question Q1 covers the idea of how effective drug therapy is and relates the answer to stimulus material.

- One example is buprenorphine which is a substitute for heroin and acts as an opioid. It has less effect than heroin and methadone so can be taken in lower doses, which do not give the withdrawal effects. The drug does not have side effects and has not caused breathing difficulties as other opiates do.
- Methadone can be more effective in someone with a strong heroin addiction as it mimics heroin more closely at the synapse.
- Li et al. (2013) (one of the contemporary studies in biological psychology) show that cues for heroin link to activation in certain brain areas (the limbic system and prefrontal cortex) and show that cues themselves affect brain functioning. So using a substitute drug might help with withdrawal and addiction, but if the cues are still there brain functioning can still be affected.

Exam tip

It is useful to note how to describe the key question as well as how to explain it using theories and concepts you have come across in your course. Also, if you learn the theories and concepts for one (or more) key question, you are likely to be able to use them if presented with an unseen key question in your exam paper.

Summary

- Learning more about drug use and drug therapy can help people to stop using drugs.
- The use of drugs can be an important issue in society for reasons from road safety to the cost of treatment or cost to the individual.
- Knowing how to treat drug abuse is useful and drug therapy, which involves prescribing a substitute drug that does not have the same addiction or withdrawal properties as the recreational drug being used has been a therapy of choice for some time (in England, the USA and other countries).
- The way drugs work at the synapse can help to explain how drug therapy works, such as the way one drug can mimic another at the synapse.
- Drug use links with environmental cues so even if the substitute drug helps with synaptic functioning as an aid to stopping use of the recreational drug, knowing that cues can cause relapse is important.

Practical investigation

You will have carried out a practical within biological psychology using correlational data. Go back over your notes to revise what you did, as it is not possible here to help you to revise that part of the course.

Some general ideas about the practical and what to learn

- Give your aim and the hypothesis, saying whether it is directional or not.
- Be sure that you are looking at aggression or attitudes to drug use.
- Be clear about the two scales you used.
- Be clear about why you asked your questions and how you gathered the data, including data collection tools.
- Understand the sampling method you used (and why).
- Understand how you dealt with ethical issues and/or how some ethical issues were not addressed and why.
- Review how you analysed the data, including using ranking, a scatter diagram and a Spearman test. Refer to the learning approach for more about testing and the Spearman test (page 53).
- Prepare material ready to evaluate your own study. Analyse using strength and direction of the correlation and doing a sense check of the data.
- Revise the results and how to write up a study, including writing up an abstract and a discussion section that includes conclusions.

Questions & Answers

Biological psychology Practical investigation Q1 gives some ideas for questions and answers about a correlation done as a practical in this topic area.

> **Exam tip**
>
> Turn these bullet points into questions and answer them, as you are likely to be asked about them. For example: 'Outline the aim of your practical and state the hypothesis for 2 marks each, and consider two ethical issues you addressed.'

> **Exam tip**
>
> You might be asked to plan a practical based on a short scenario. Use your understanding of methodology from your own practical to devise a different one.

Summary

- The practical has to be such that correlational analysis can take place and must focus on aggression or attitudes to drug use.
- Ethical principles must be followed.
- Descriptive statistics must be used to analyse the data, which for a correlation will be the strength of the correlation (how close to +1 or −1) and the direction (positive or negative).
- There must be inferential statistical testing including using Spearman's rho, explaining the significance of the result and using level of significance.
- The data are to be commented on as well, which can include evaluation of your study. You need an abstract and a discussion section including conclusions.
- In the study you must include a research question/hypothesis, the research method, sampling, ethical considerations, data-collection tools, data analysis, results and a discussion.

Issues and debates (A-level only)

If you are studying for the AS, you do not need to know about issues and debates.

To help A-level students to become familiar with the 11 'issues and debates' ready for their Topic 9 section, they are explained at the end of each topic area and they are reviewed here with biological psychology in mind.

Issues and debates in psychology	Links to biological psychology in your course
Ethical issues in research	Ethics are important when researching in psychology, including adoption studies. Leve et al. (2010) as part of the EDGS study had to maintain confidentiality between birth mothers and birth fathers, for example. The content that is studied can also bring ethical issues such as research into aggression showing links with brain damage.
Practical issues in research	There are many research methods — many with practical issues in biological psychology in your course. Scanning is not something that can be done without the equipment, for example, and participants have to be in the right place, unlike, perhaps, doing a questionnaire. The brain is hard to measure anyway, being so complex, and even up-to-date scanning methods cannot measure all that is required. Twin studies are hard to do as MZ and DZ twins have to be found. One practical issue is that it is not easy to get information about whether twins are identical or non-identical.
Reductionism	Reducing aggression to brain structures is likely to miss studying the whole person. For example, the prefrontal cortex is implicated in aggression but is thought to be about control so it would mean damage to that area removes control and might lead to aggression. This is far from saying that this area causes all aggression. **Reductionism** is reducing what is studied into parts and the issue is that perhaps **holism** (looking at the whole) is better as it is more valid (more real).
Explaining using different themes	The psychodynamic and biological explanations of aggression can be compared and contrasted — these use different themes and concepts.
Psychology as a science	Synaptic transmission is biology, and brain scanning is scientific, using a radioactive tracer, for example.
Cultural and gender issues in research	Culture is not covered in this topic area in your course. Gender is mentioned, such as showing that Brendgen et al. in their twin study did not find gender differences. The study of gender and culture directly, though, is not covered.
Nature-nurture	Mostly this topic area is focusing on nature and our inherited characteristics, when it comes to discussing the **nature–nurture debate**. For example, frustration is said to link to aggression, but biological psychology does not consider interactions between people for the most part — biological psychology is about hormones, neurotransmitters and brain structure, which are innate. There are, however, environmental influences that are considered, such as Brendgen et al.'s twin study looking at peer judgement of aggression in the twins.
Development over time	Scanning has developed over time, from MRI to fMRI, for example. The availability of scanning has improved, and so more findings from scanning as a research method are available.
Social control	Raine et al. (1997) looked at evidence that was being produced to show that people were not guilty by reason of insanity — perhaps because of brain differences and so any aggression on their part would be outside their control. Society can use such evidence as a form of social control, albeit in this case to help people perhaps, as they might not then be charged with murder. They would, however, be controlled in some way, such as in a mental institution.
Use of psychology within society	Knowing how recreational drugs work in the brain has led to drug therapies such as substitute drugs being used in place of heroin. These drugs do not have the addictive qualities of heroin or give the same withdrawal symptoms. This helps society. Knowing more about the causes of aggression can also help society.
Socially sensitive research	Research in biological psychology can be socially sensitive, including Raine et al.'s study (or more accurately the data they used is socially sensitive).

Table 20 Issues and debates and how biological psychology illustrates each

Biological psychology Content Q2 considers whether the psychodynamic approach is unscientific.

Exam tip

The 11 issues and debates are repeated at the end of each topic area to show how that topic area illustrates them. Make notes for each issue and debate, drawing together all the ideas in the topic areas, so that you have a wide range of examples of that issue/debate.

Summary: biological psychology

- Biological psychology includes studying neurotransmitter functioning, synaptic transmission and the central nervous system.
- Recreational drugs work at the synapse.
- Brain structure and functioning, related to aggression, is covered (e.g. the role of the prefrontal cortex).
- An alternative to biological ideas is the psychodynamic explanation for aggression, including the three parts of the personality, the importance of the unconscious and catharsis.
- Hormones take messages that affect brain functioning, though in a way that is different from neurotransmitter functioning, and hormones can help to explain behaviour such as aggression.
- Individual differences are looked at when Freud considers the personality and when brain damage is different in different individuals.

- Development is considered by looking at evolution ideas and at the role of hormones.
- Methods covered in biological psychology include correlation, brain scanning and twin and adoption studies. Analysis uses inferential statistics, with a focus on the Spearman's test and related issues such as levels of measurement. Experiments are also revisited, to compare their features with the features of correlations.
- The classic study is Raine et al. (1997) and the chosen contemporary study included here is Brendgen et al. (2005).
- The chosen key question is: How effective is drug therapy for treating addictions?
- There is a practical investigation which must generate data that can be analysed using correlational analysis.

■ Learning theories

This section looks at learning theories with its five main parts (content; method; studies; key question; practical investigation) and also an issues and debates section. In some places in your course you can choose what you study. In this section suitable material is presented, but you may have studied different examples (this is indicated). *You might be better advised to revise the material you chose for your course.*

Content

The main features of classical conditioning including main terms. These are unconditioned stimulus, unconditioned response, conditioned stimulus, neutral stimulus, conditioned response. Also extinction, spontaneous recovery and stimulus generalisation are covered. Pavlov's work with dogs (1927) links to classical conditioning.

The main features of operant conditioning including main terms. These are types of reinforcement and punishment (positive and negative), properties of reinforcement including primary, secondary and schedules of reinforcement. Also behaviour modification including shaping, which uses operant conditioning principles.

The main features of social learning theory including main terms. These are observation, imitation, modelling and vicarious reinforcement. There are stages to social learning as well — attention, retention, reproduction and motivation (reinforcement). Bandura (with others) carried out studies in 1961, 1963 and 1965 (his study on vicarious reinforcement) and you need to cover all three studies.

How learning theories explain acquiring and maintaining phobias, as well as looking at treatments for phobias based on learning theories including systematic desensitisation and one other treatment.

As in other topic areas individual differences and developmental psychology need to be linked into the content studied.

Methodology

Observational research method, including gathering both qualitative and quantitative data (tallying, event and time sampling). Types of observation — participant, non-participant, overt and covert as well as structured and naturalistic observations.

Content analysis as a research method. Analysis of qualitative data using thematic analysis.

Using animals in laboratory experiments and relating findings to humans, as well as the ethics involved in using animals in this way — Animals (Scientific Procedures) Act (1986) and Home Office regulations.

Inferential statistics including levels of measurement, reasons for choosing the chi-squared test, looking at observed and critical values, and levels of significance — and the chi-squared test itself.

Finally, the scientific status of psychology including replicability, reliability, validity (internal, predictive and ecological), reductionism, falsification, empiricism, hypothesis testing and use of controls.

Two studies in detail

Watson and Rayner (1920) and Becker et al. (2002) are described and evaluated. You may have studied Capafóns et al. (1998) or Bastian et al. (2011) instead.

Key question

The question of whether the influence of role models and celebrities is something that causes anorexia nervosa is given here, but you may have looked at one or more different key questions.

Practical

You will have carried out at least one practical within learning theories and you should use your own practical, because you will have 'learned by doing'. Some ideas about the practical are suggested in this book.

Issues and debates*

Unless you are studying at AS, there are 11 issues and debates in your course: ethics; practical issues in the design and implementation of research; reductionism; comparisons of ways of explaining behaviour using different themes; psychology as a science; culture and gender; nature-nurture; understanding of how psychological understanding has developed over time; issues of social control; the use of psychological knowledge in society; issues related to socially sensitive research.
Issues and debates are not required at AS, but they can be useful for evaluation purposes.

Table 21 Summary of learning theories in your course

Use Table 21 to draw up a checklist of what you need to cover. Annotate it to show what you feel you know, what just needs some brief revision and which areas you need to focus on.

Which learning theory suggests that learning is by imitating others? Which two learning theories use the idea of reinforcement as part of their ideas? Which learning theory is about learning associations between stimuli?

Learning theories focus on environmental influences on us — nurture. In a way this is the opposite from biological psychology which is about nature and our biology. Learning theories focus on how we are conditioned to behave in certain ways and how we tend to repeat behaviour that we are rewarded for. We also learn from watching others, particularly if they are rewarded.

Exam tip

Be ready for questions that ask you about the learning approach in general, such as focusing on the effects of the environment and nurture, or how reinforcement processes guide behaviour.

Questions & Answers

Learning theories Overview Q1 gives an example for each of the three learning theories in your course — classical conditioning, operant conditioning and social learning theory.

Classical conditioning

Pavlov is the main person associated with classical conditioning, so an example from his studies is given here.

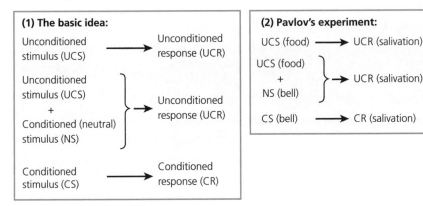

Figure 5 Classical conditioning

The **unconditioned stimulus** gives an **involuntary response**, called the **unconditioned response**. 'Involuntary' means a reflex response, not a deliberate

Exam tip

Make sure that you can fit the main features into a diagram like this if you are given one in the exam (features are UCS, UCR, NS, CS, CR). A diagram can be presented as an exam question, where you have to complete it.

one. Then a **neutral stimulus** is paired with the unconditioned stimulus, still giving the unconditioned response. When the association has taken place (after a few pairings) the neutral stimulus is a **conditioned stimulus** because it gives the **conditioned response**.

Other features of classical conditioning

Extinction occurs when the association (for example, between the bell and the food) is no longer presented. After a while the response (salivation) no longer occurs when the stimulus (the bell) appears.

Spontaneous recovery is the term for when, after extinction, a previously conditioned association (for example, salivating to the sound of a bell) reoccurs without more conditioning. The response to the stimulus reoccurs spontaneously.

Stimulus generalisation is when the neutral stimulus, which becomes the conditioned stimulus, is not used exactly but still elicits the response. For example, salivating to the sound of a bell but not the original bell.

Questions & Answers

Learning theories Content Q1 defines extinction and spontaneous recovery.

Links

Developmental psychology link

Learning through classical conditioning affects someone's development in that they might develop a phobia, for example, and they will develop associations between stimuli and reflexive responses.

Pavlov's (1927) experiment with dogs

Pavlov did a series of experiments, which were explained in his 1927 lectures. He showed how a dog would salivate when food was in its mouth and noticed that the salivation response can be associated with a new stimulus (not the food). This was classical conditioning.

Pavlov used a metronome, paired with meat, and eventually the metronome gave salivation. He also used an electric buzzer, again finding the association was learned by the dog.

Aims

Pavlov wanted to know how the cerebral cortex works and he chose dogs because they have some higher-order thinking and yet are manageable. He wanted to look at reflex behaviour to see if he could work out pathways to the brain.

Procedure

Pavlov realised from looking at what others were doing (e.g. Thorndike) that he needed to be scientific in his work so he started noting everything down. His 1927 lectures summarised 25 years of his work with 100 or so collaborators. He quickly discovered that the cerebral cortex is needed for survival, not just reflexes (dogs with damage to the cerebral cortex would not survive in spite of reflexes being intact). There must be some thinking going on.

Pavlov chose salivation as it is measurable (drops can be counted or the amount can be seen in a glass tube). The researchers found that even the stimuli from one experimenter led to associations and learning, e.g. the blink of an eye, or sweating. So they had to build a special chamber for the dog where the dog would not even hear footsteps. Pavlov and the researchers carried out their many experiments by varying the stimulus that was to be paired with the unconditioned stimulus. Pavlov thought that the pairing had to take place about 20 times but he did find variations in this. Pavlov felt that the salivation to the meat was a reflex, but when the association is made between the metronome beat and salivation this must affect higher-order thinking and there must be new paths made in the cortex.

Results

In the study using the metronome, salivation starts after 9 seconds and by 45 seconds 11 drops were collected (Lecture II). There were of course other results. For example, there could be secondary conditioning, such as if the metronome is paired with a buzzer (after the metronome is associated with salivation) then the buzzer will give salivation.

Conclusions

Pavlov thought that 'signalisation' in the brain links the metronome to the food and gives the salivation response. In a natural environment the dog would salivate to meat but would have to find meat so learning to salivate to a stimulus such as the smell of the meat would be useful. Pavlov also found that not all dogs were the same — the same experiment done on two different dogs can have a different result. He found as well that there were factors external to the experiment that affected the conditioning.

Strengths	Weaknesses
His studies used experimental method and controls so were scientific and cause-and-effect conclusions could be drawn	Studies use animals, so generalisability and credibility are in doubt
He and his colleagues carried out many experiments and found the same result — that a stimulus could be conditioned into producing a reflex, so there was reliability in his findings	Studies are laboratory experiments and use animals, so validity is in doubt

Table 22 Strengths and weaknesses of Pavlov (1927)

Operant conditioning

Another type of conditioning is operant conditioning. Some features of operant conditioning are given in Table 23.

Feature of operant conditioning	Explanation
Positive reinforcement	Something good is given because of the behaviour, so the behaviour is repeated.
Negative reinforcement	Something bad is taken away because of the behaviour and so the behaviour is repeated.
Positive punishment	Something bad/undesired is given and the unwanted behaviour is stopped.
Negative punishment	Something good/desired is taken away and the unwanted behaviour is stopped.
Primary reinforcement	The reward is a basic need, like food or warmth.
Secondary reinforcement	The reward is something that can buy or get a basic need, like money or tokens.
Schedules of reinforcement	■ Fixed interval schedule is when the reward (or punishment) is at a fixed time (e.g. every 5 minutes). ■ Variable interval schedule is when reward (or punishment) is varied regarding the time (e.g. first at 2 minutes, then 5 minutes later...). ■ Fixed ratio is a reward (or punishment) every so many responses (e.g. reward every 3 times you hand in homework). ■ Variable ratio is a reward (or punishment) given when different numbers of responses are achieved (e.g. after 3 responses, then 7, then 1...).
Behaviour modification	If rewards (or punishments) are planned, so that certain behaviours are produced and others are dropped, this is modifying the individual's behaviour.
Shaping	One way of modifying behaviour is to use shaping. Shaping means gradually working towards the required behaviour by rewards or punishments. For example, to get a pigeon to turn a circle you could reward small turns, then larger ones until you just reward a complete turn.

Table 23 Features of operant conditioning

Links

Developmental psychology link

Learning through operant conditioning affects someone's development in that society uses shaping, for example, to encourage required behaviour. An example is rewarding good work in school or punishing behaviour that is not environmentally friendly by charging for bags in a shop.

Individual differences link

Learning through operant conditioning principles, and classical conditioning principles too, leads to people reacting differently to certain stimuli in the environment and in that way individual differences in behaviour can develop.

Exam tip

The terms included in Table 23 are the key terms in operant conditioning, so you might be asked about any of them specifically. Use the specification to check on words (e.g. 'punishment', 'primary reinforcement') that are likely to appear in exam questions.

Knowledge check 15

Give two differences between negative punishment and negative reinforcement.

Strengths	Weaknesses
Studies use experimental method and controls so they are scientific and cause-and-effect conclusions can be drawn	Studies use animals, so generalisability and credibility are in doubt
Both can be applied in therapies and so they have practical applications	Studies are laboratory experiments and use animals, so validity is in doubt

Table 24 Strengths and weaknesses of operant and classical conditioning as explanations of human behaviour

Social learning

The third learning theory you need to know about is **social learning theory**. Features of the theory are:

- Children and others learn from **role models** — people looked up to and identified with.
- Social learning theory is **observational learning**. The behaviour of role models is observed in particular.
- After the behaviour is observed it is then **imitated**.
- Social learning theory involves cognitive elements — behaviour is modelled. To be imitated it needs to be observed, attended to (attention), stored in memory (retention) and rewarded so that there is motivation (motivation using reinforcement) to reproduce it (reproduction).
- Whether the behaviour is repeated depends on various issues such as whether the role model was rewarded for the behaviour, and whether the observer identifies with the model (e.g. being the same gender or similar in some other way).
- **'Vicarious learning'** is behaviour that is carried out because of seeing someone else carry it out and seeing them being rewarded for it. 'Vicarious' means not direct.

Links

Developmental psychology link

As with the other two learning theories, social learning theory can be seen to explain how humans develop. In the case of social learning this is through watching others be rewarded or punished for doing something, and reacting accordingly, or through copying role models, those who are admired.

Strengths	Weaknesses
There is a great deal of experimental evidence to support the theory and the behaviour that is learned is visible, so the evidence is strong	There might be a lack of validity as the behaviour might not be exhibited immediately, so it might be thought that no learning had taken place, when, in fact, it had
The theory gives rise to practical applications such as in therapy and in explaining, for example, why violence on television or in media games might be copied	Studies are often carried out on animals and it can be difficult to generalise to humans from animal studies

Table 25 Strengths and weaknesses of social learning as an explanation of human behaviour

Exam tip

You will need to evaluate learning theories. When evaluating a theory you could: think of an **a**lternative theory for 1 mark (explain why it is different) (**A**); evaluate the **m**ethodology used in developing/testing the theory (**M**); give **e**vidence for the theory or against it (**E**) (studies that people have done); consider practical **a**pplications that have arisen from the theory (**A**).

Exam tip

Check the specification to see the particular areas of social learning theory that you need to know about. Learn definitions of key terms — not just the key terms listed in the specification, but key terms used in the theory, such as 'role model'.

Bandura, Ross and Ross (1961)

Aims

To see whether young children imitate behaviour that they have seen. One specific aim was to see the effect of the gender of the role model and the gender of the observing child.

Procedure

Use a textbook or some other source to remind yourself of the details in the procedure for this study. It is useful to learn the procedure carefully as elements of it are found in the 1963/1965 studies too.

Results/conclusions

In the non-aggressive condition little aggressive behaviour was recorded and around 70% of the children showed no aggression at all. In the aggressive condition a lot of the adult's behaviour was seen, including both the verbal and physical aggression. Girls in the non-aggressive condition performed on average 0.5 aggressive acts with the mallet, whereas in the aggressive condition an average of 18 aggressive acts with the mallet were observed in girls. About 13 aggressive acts with the mallet were observed in the girls in the control condition, so it is thought that modelling non-aggressive behaviour leads to less aggression. There were many other findings, such as that in general the boys were more aggressive than the girls, although girls tended to show verbal aggression. It was in physical terms that the girls were less aggressive.

Strengths	Weaknesses
The study has controls with operationalisation of variables, so cause-and-effect conclusions can be drawn; for example, the aggressive acts were set up so that they could be observed later	The situation was not natural; the children might have thought that they were supposed to hit the Bobo doll, given that they had seen adults doing it
There is reliability because two judges observed the behaviour and their scores could be compared; one judge did not know to which condition a child had been allocated, so was not biased	The study might not be ethical because children observed verbal and physical aggressive acts and repeated them; how ethical issues were dealt with was not clearly explained

Table 26 Strengths and weaknesses of Bandura et al. (1961)

Links

Individual differences link

It could be said that learning theories go against individual differences in that people are shaped by the environment, which can be largely the same for individuals in one culture. However, individual differences do occur because individuals react differently, such as individual differences around gender, where boys and girls imitate differently depending on the gender of a model.

Exam tip

You have to know three of the Bandura studies (1961, 1963, 1965) so find a way of distinguishing them so you can remember which is which. A good way is to note down the different independent variables as they are the key difference.

Bandura, Ross and Ross (1963)

Use a textbook or other source to find out about the aims and procedure of this study, which was about imitation of film-mediated aggressive models. A lot of this study builds on the 1961 study.

The 1961 study looked at gender and whether the children saw an aggressive or a non-aggressive model. The 1963 study looks at three conditions — a human model, a film of the human model or a cartoon model.

Results

Mean total real-life aggression	Mean total human film aggression	Mean total cartoon aggression	Mean total control group aggression
83	92	99	54

Table 27 The mean total aggression scores for the three conditions and the control group

Table 27 shows that the control group's aggression (mean average) was nearly half that of the 'cartoon' aggression and a lot lower than the 'real life' and 'film' aggression tool.

There were other results as well, such as those who observed the real-life or film conditions showed a lot more imitative physical and verbal aggression that those in the control group. The highest total aggression score was for boys imitating the real-life male model (131.8 aggressive acts) and the lowest (excluding the control condition, where the girls showed the lowest aggression —36.4 aggressive acts) was girls imitating the real-life male model (57.3 aggressive acts). The boys showed more aggression compared with the girls, looking at total aggression as the measure, in all the conditions.

Conclusions

The researchers concluded that observing filmed aggression (and real-life aggression) will lead to aggressive acts in children. It was also clear that watching the aggression was not cathartic as Freud may have claimed (page 17). The actual aggressive acts were copied as well, so not only is watching aggression likely to give aggression but the type of aggression is likely to be shown too.

Strengths	Weaknesses
The study has controls with operationalisation of variables, so cause-and-effect conclusions can be drawn; for example, the aggressive acts were set up so that they could be observed later	The situation was not natural; the children might have thought that they were supposed to hit the Bobo doll, given that they had seen adults doing it
The findings can be applied to help society and have been, as violence on television is now controlled so that children are protected from watching it	The study might not be generalisable because the sample used US children from one university nursery and they might not be representative of 'all children'

Table 28 Strengths and weaknesses of Bandura et al. (1963)

Bandura (1965)

This study is similar to the 1961 and 1963 studies. This time Bandura focuses on the reinforcement side of the aggression and how that might affect the children's imitation of aggression they watch. Use a textbook or other source to find out about the aims and procedure of this study.

In one condition in this 1965 study the model is punished for showing physical and verbal aggression, in one condition the model is rewarded and in a third condition there are no consequences. Bandura thought that seeing a model rewarded would lead to more imitative aggression than if there were no consequences and seeing a model punished would lead to less imitative aggression than if there were no consequences. There was also a condition where the child was directly rewarded with a sticker and more juice if they reproduced the aggressive acts, and it was thought that a direct reward would be more reinforcing than watching a model being rewarded.

Results

The direct reward of juice and a sticker did lead to more imitative aggression than any of the other conditions (model rewarded, model punished, no consequence). This was the case both for boys and girls. In the three modelled conditions (model rewarded, model punished, no consequence) the boys showed most aggressive acts compared with the girls. For boys the lowest mean imitative acts was when the model was punished and for both girls and boys the condition when the model was punished showed the least imitative acts.

Conclusions

It appears that watching aggression that is punished does deter someone from imitating that behaviour. Bandura concluded that many variables were involved in whether a behaviour is imitated or not, including the consequences of the aggression for the person carrying it out. If someone is not motivated to carry out an act they have seen (because the act was punished) that affects whether they imitate the act or not. Variables include the gender of the observer and the consequences for the model of the aggression.

> **Exam tip**
>
> Note that as Bandura, Ross and Ross (1963) is a continuation of the 1961 study, the evaluation points can be the same.

Strengths	Weaknesses
The study has controls with operationalisation of variables, so cause-and-effect conclusions can be drawn; for example, the aggressive acts were set up so that they could be observed later	The situation was not natural; there were many other variables that might in real life affect whether a modelled act is imitated or not and the study, by isolating certain variables (e.g. whether the model was rewarded, punished or there were no consequences) the validity is likely to have been compromised
The findings can be applied to help society and have been, as violence on television is now controlled so that children are protected from watching it	The study might not be generalisable because the sample used US children from one university nursery and they might not be representative of 'all children'

Table 29 Strengths and weaknesses of Bandura (1965)

> **Knowledge check 17**
>
> Show how the independent variables are different in the 1961, 1963 and 1965 studies.

Phobias: acquisition, maintenance, treatments

Acquisition and maintenance of phobias

Classical conditioning, operant conditioning and social learning theory can all explain the acquisition and maintenance of phobias.

Classical conditioning

Watson and Rayner's (1920) study of Little Albert (pages 58–59) shows how classical conditioning principles can be used to give someone a **phobia** (a fear response that affects normal functioning). A fear response to a neutral **stimulus** arises when the neutral stimulus is paired with an unconditioned stimulus. In the case of Little Albert his fear **response** to a loud noise was replaced by a fear response to the pet rat by pairing the playing of the rat with the loud noise to form an association.

Classical conditioning principles can be used to maintain the phobia. It is likely that the pairing between the unconditioned stimulus and neutral stimulus would have to be renewed occasionally, as was the case in Watson and Rayner's (1920) study.

Operant conditioning

A phobia can be conditioned and operant conditioning principles can explain this conditioning. For example, if a fear of something is rewarded, perhaps by someone getting attention, then that response is likely to be repeated. It might be that negative consequences to an action lead to the phobia. That would mean learning through negative reinforcement, which means avoiding something that causes pain or fear. This could be how the fear becomes a phobia, which is when the fear interferes with normal functioning.

Avoiding the fear, which might occur through negative reinforcement, is not likely to lead to overcoming it, as the opportunity for rewarding facing the fear is not there. This is how the phobia can be maintained.

Social learning

Bandura showed (1961, 1963, 1965) that children learned to imitate what they watched. If a role model shows fear of something (a phobia) then someone might imitate that behaviour. If the fear is punished, then the observer might not show that behaviour through observational learning, but often a fear is not punished, so that type of vicarious learning would not occur. Lieb et al. (2000) found children of parents with social phobia were likely to have social phobia themselves, which supports the idea that phobias can be acquired and maintained through social learning.

Strengths	Weaknesses
The studies that the conditioning theories rest on have controls with operationalisation of variables, so cause-and-effect conclusions can be drawn	The conditioning theories are drawn mainly from animal studies and humans have consciousness, emotions and thinking that go beyond that of animals
There is reliability in Bandura's work because two judges observed the behaviour and their scores could be compared; one judge did not know to which condition a child had been allocated, so was not biased — this too shows that evidence for the theory is strong so practical applications seem justified	The evidence for the theories tends to come from a reductionist approach to study, whereas phobias involve the whole person

Table 30 Strengths and weaknesses of how learning theories explain phobias

One treatment for phobias from classical conditioning: systematic desensitisation

Systematic desensitisation, developed by Wolpe in 1958, is used to help or cure phobias using principles of classical conditioning. The example of a spider phobia explains the treatment. The aim is to replace the phobia of spiders with a new association, 'lack of fear'. This lack of fear is **operationalised** (made measurable and useful) as relaxation. The treatment is to desensitise the individual so they are no longer sensitive to (have a phobia of) spiders; and it is systematic because it is in steps.

The first step is to teach the person deep muscle relaxation, so that they can achieve the desired relaxed response. The next step is gradually to introduce the idea of spiders while the person relaxes. Then a picture of a spider is introduced, still with relaxation. The final step is a real spider, with the person being taught to stay relaxed. In this way the person is systematically (step-by-step) desensitised (taught not to be afraid).

Strengths	Weaknesses
It is more ethical than other therapies for phobias (e.g. flooding) because it involves a gradual exposure to phobic objects or situations and individuals are involved fully in their therapy	Not everyone can learn to relax and take such a central part in therapy; it is only useful for some mental health issues, and not, for example, for psychoses
Studies show that the therapy is successful (e.g. Capafóns et al. 1998 showed that it helped to overcome a fear of flying)	There are issues such as operant conditioning principles and cognitive processes being involved, so the explanation — resting on classical conditioning — is not the whole story

Table 31 Strengths and weaknesses of systematic desensitisation as a treatment for phobias

Learning theories Content Q2 assesses systematic desensitisation as a therapy for phobias and should help in understanding how to 'assess' in the examination.

Exam tip

If you are studying the A-level course, you will find that theories and therapies are returned to, including both classical and operant conditioning. For example, for the psychological skills part of your course (Topic 9), systematic desensitisation can be used as an example of social control using classical conditioning.

One treatment for phobias from classical conditioning: flooding

Flooding is a treatment for phobias that is also called 'exposure therapy'. This therapy rests on classical conditioning principles, as does systematic desensitisation. The idea is to replace the fear response with a non-fear response, but the process is different from systematic desensitisation.

The idea is that someone can only experience heightened alertness for a short time, and then the physical requirements to maintain the alarm reaction are not going to be there (e.g. blood sugar). This means that an alarm reaction, as happens in a phobia, is not going to be maintained for long. This is the biological part of the theory behind this treatment.

If someone is exposed to their fear object, they will have the fear response, as explained through classical conditioning principles. However, the fear response will not last. When the fear response dies out, the individual will interpret that as replacing their fear response with a calm response. The neutral stimulus (the fear object) would then give a calm response and not a fear response.

An example of using flooding

Figure 6 shows how a phobia might be developed through classical conditioning.

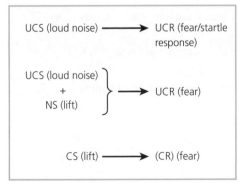

Figure 6 Developing a phobia through classical conditioning

Using flooding to help with this phobia

The lift gives the fear so someone is put into a lift and left there — they are exposed to their fear object. Over time the fear response will die out, using the biological explanation given above. So the fear reaction to the lift then becomes a calm reaction to being in the lift and the phobia is helped/cured.

Strengths	Weaknesses
The treatment can be frightening and perhaps not ethical. Systematic desensitisation with its focus on gradual exposure to the feared object seems less distressing	There can be spontaneous recovery and the effectiveness of the treatment may be short lived
The underpinning theory seems to be well evidenced and this strengthens the claims for the therapy	If flooding involves the individual using their imagination (e.g. reliving their fears) then this brings in a cognitive element, and perhaps there is more to flooding than pure behaviourism
There is evidence for effectiveness, such as Wolpe (1973)	

Table 32 Strengths and weaknesses of flooding as a treatment for phobias

Knowledge check 20

Compare systematic desensitisation and flooding as treatments for a phobia.

Individual differences

In the content sections for learning theories the importance of individual differences in people has been noted. Here is a summary:

■ Operant and classical conditioning can lead to individual differences because different people are shaped in different ways to respond to stimuli and they learn different associations.

■ Social learning can show individual differences, for example, boys and girls in Bandura et al.'s (1961) study imitated aggression differently depending on the gender of the model.

Developmental psychology

In the content sections for learning theories the importance of issues for our development has been noted. Here is a summary:

■ Classical conditioning shows how associations between stimuli and responses are learned and affect someone's development. They may learn a phobia that way, for example.

■ Operant conditioning shows how we develop through patterns of reward and punishment.

■ Social learning theory emphasises the role of role models on our development.

Summary

- Learning theories include three main theories: classical conditioning, operant conditioning and social learning theory.
- The main features of classical conditioning are the unconditioned and conditioned stimuli, the unconditioned and conditioned responses and the neutral stimulus. Also extinction, spontaneous recovery and stimulus generalisation are involved.
- The main features of operant conditioning are positive and negative reinforcement and positive and negative punishment. Also primary and secondary reinforcement, schedules of reinforcement and behaviour modification (including shaping) are important.
- The main features of social learning theory are observation, imitation, modelling and vicarious reinforcement. Also 'stages' of social learning — attention, retention, reproduction and motivation (reinforcement).
- As well as the three main theories of learning you need to look at two researchers in some detail. For classical conditioning you need to study Pavlov's (1927) experiments with salivation in dogs and for social learning theory you need to study Bandura's work. For Bandura's work you need to cover his original Bobo doll studies (1961, 1963) and the 1965 experiment looking at vicarious reinforcement.
- You also need to know how learning theories explain both the acquisition and maintenance of phobias, as well as two learning-based treatments for phobias including systematic desensitisation and one other.
- Alongside the main content you need to learn about, you need to make notes about where individual differences are covered in learning theories — people's different experiences and environmental influences in rewards, punishments and models observed, for example, can lead to individual differences.
- Developmental psychology also needs to be noted, though as learning theories are about how people develop — such as focusing on developing through patterns of rewards and punishments as well as by observing others — this whole topic area is about how people develop.

Method

- One of the new research methods you need to learn for the learning approach is observation — this is featured first in this section.
- Issues you need for doing inferential statistical analysis are also summarised here — they have all been left until this section rather than some being covered in the biological approach. This section just has a summary of issues in inferential statistics as *Edexcel Psychology: Social psychology and cognitive psychology (with issues and debates) Student Guide* covers these in more detail.
- Analysis of qualitative data using thematic analysis needs to be known about too.
- You also need to know about content analysis as a research method. This is outlined after looking at observations.
- Laboratory experiments with animals is the other method you need to consider here — including ethical issues when using animals in experiments.
- Finally, issues about psychology and science are covered.

Human research

In this section two research methods using humans as participants are considered: observations and content analysis.

Exam tip

You need to know the terms: participant, non-participant, covert, overt and naturalistic/structured observations. Think of a few examples of observations for each methodology, so that you can illustrate your answer if asked to explain what a term means.

Observations

Features of **observations** are explained briefly in Table 33.

	Covert (secret)	Overt (open and known about)
Participant	Observer takes part and the study is not known about.	Observer takes part and the study is known about.
Non-participant	Observer does not take part and the study is not known about.	Observer does not take part and the study is known about.
Structured	In the observation the situation is set up and then what happens is observed (can also be naturalistic, overt, covert, participant, non-participant)	
Naturalistic	The observation takes place in the participant's natural setting (can also be structured, overt, covert, participant, non-participant)	

Table 33 Features of observations as a research method

Knowledge check 21

Which type of observation (naturalistic or structured) is it when the participants know that there is a study going on and the researcher is someone they do not know, who is not part of the group?

Questions & Answers

Learning theories Method Q1 is a 12-mark essay question about evaluating observation as a research method so can help your learning of this area.

Type of observation	Strengths	Weaknesses
Covert observations	■ The behaviour of the participants is likely to be natural because they are unaware that they are being observed; therefore, there is **validity** ■ The observation is easier because the observer can carry out the study without the participants watching what the observer is doing	■ They are often not ethical because there is no informed consent; if they are not carried out in a public place, they go against ethical guidelines ■ The observer cannot be helped by the participants (e.g. to find a suitable place for observation) because the participants are unaware that the study is taking place
Overt observations	■ They are ethical because informed consent can be gained and the right to withdraw can be given ■ Observers can ask for help to set up the study (e.g. where to observe from)	■ The participants know that they are being watched so might not act in a natural way. Therefore, there is doubt about validity of the data ■ It might be difficult to carry out because the observers themselves would be watched to see what they are doing
Participant observations	■ There is **ecological validity** because the observation is in the natural setting, including not having a stranger present ■ A participant observer is likely to gather valid data because the setting is natural and what occurs is also natural	■ The observer may be too involved to record all the data, partly because they cannot step back from the situation and partly because they have another role ■ They are difficult to replicate because it is not easy to find an observer who is also a member of the group
Non-participant observations	■ Non-participant observers are **objective**. They can stand back from the situation better than participant observers ■ Non-participant observers can record data more easily than participant observers because they have the time to concentrate ■ They can use time-sampling when tallying, which might be difficult when participating and observing at the same time	■ Non-participant observers are likely to affect the situation just by their presence ■ Non-participant observers might miss the relevance of some interactions or might misunderstand something, whereas participant observers have the advantage of shared understanding with the participants

Type of observation	Strengths	Weaknesses
Structured	■ Structured observations are set up and can be repeated — so results can be compared between observations and **reliability** is likely ■ This is a way to ensure that the behaviour to be observed does take place — it can take a long time for some behaviours to occur naturally	■ The situation is set up and so is artificial in some ways, suggesting a lack of ecological validity ■ It is possible that the situation, though set up carefully, might be interpreted differently by different participants so it may not be as controlled as might be thought
Naturalistic	■ Observations take place in the natural environment of the participant, so there is ecological validity ■ They gather much in-depth data and detail, which is difficult using any other research method; data are often **qualitative** and rich; even when **quantitative**, the data can be detailed	■ There might be **subjectivity** because the observer has to choose what to observe and what to record ■ An observation is of one group or individual at one moment in time, so the data are not **generalisable** to other people at different times

Table 34 Strengths and weaknesses of different types of observation

Questions & Answers

Learning theories Method Q2 asks questions about an unseen observation study. This should help you to see how to answer such questions and learn more about observations.

Exam tip

Giving the strengths and weaknesses of the various types of observation includes using the following terms: validity, reliability, generalisability, subjectivity, objectivity, ethics. Make sure you understand clearly what each means.

Qualitative and quantitative data

■ Qualitative data are gathered in the form of a story or words, such as writing down how a child is playing.
■ Quantitative data are gathered in the form of numbers, such as finding out how often a child in a nursery goes outside to play.

Tallying, event sampling, time sampling

■ **Tallying:** making a mark on a piece of paper or somehow, to record each instance of something happening, such as someone holding a door open for another person with shopping in a busy shopping centre.
■ **Event sampling:** choosing which events are to be observed and then noting down each time that event occurs. Watching instances of door-holding for people with shopping is an example of event sampling.
■ **Time sampling:** observing for certain periods of time, perhaps every 5 minutes, with then a 5-minute break, before observing for another 5 minutes. This can make observations manageable.

Knowledge check 22

Which type of observation has the strength of being able to be objective because the observer can focus on the task more than if using a different type of observation?

Exam tip

You will have carried out an observation when doing your practical— or possibly two observations as you need to collect qualitative and quantitative data. You are likely to have used tallying and possibly time and event sampling, so draw on that understanding when answering questions about these features of observations.

Content analysis

Content analysis is a method of gathering data. The 'content' is from articles, newspapers, media programmes, books — auditory or visual material. Content analysis involves going through texts or other sources to find key terms or instances, generating categories. Coding is done.

There are three types of content analysis:

- **Conventional content analysis:** picking categories out from the data (e.g. looking to see how mental health is mentioned in the media and generating categories, without theory in mind).
- **Directive content analysis:** theory drives the categories (e.g. looking for right-wing authoritarian traits).
- **Summative content analysis:** searching for key words and then counting them (or references to an issue), before interpreting the data.

Qualitative data are gathered from content analysis if the data are formed into a story/text about categories/issues, such as writing about how mental health is understood in the media. There can also be tallying of categories/issues (e.g. counting the number of times the sun is drawn in children's drawings), which would give quantitative data.

If there is more than one person doing the content analysis there can be **inter-researcher reliability**. Note that observations can be done by more than one researcher too, and if the findings are the same, then there is **inter-observer reliability**.

Strengths	Weaknesses
The research method is ethical as it uses secondary sources such as articles in magazines, newspapers and other media or information from television programmes. Participants are not involved and there are few problems with informed consent, for example (although the source for the data must be chosen carefully and consent to use material may be needed)	The research method is limited to the study of existing articles and media sources, which means it is inflexible and specialist. It is useful on certain occasions but those occasions are limited
Content analyses are also reliable, because someone else can go to the same source or sources and repeat the analysis, tallying using the same categories. There can be inter-researcher reliability	The categories have to be chosen and defined by the researcher(s), which might bring in subjectivity — someone has to decide what is a 'female' and a 'male' role, and people might differ in their opinions

Table 35 Strengths and weaknesses of content analysis

Animal research

You need to know about the use of animals in laboratory experiments where results can be related to humans and about ethical issues in the use of animals in laboratory research.

Exam tip

For A-level, in clinical psychology you will carry out a summative content analysis to look at attitudes to mental health. You will be taking Paper 1, which learning theories relates to, at the end of your second year. By then you will have covered clinical psychology, so you will have done a content analysis.

Knowledge check 23

How can content analysis be made reliable?

The use of animals in laboratory experiments

Revise all that you have learned about laboratory experiments, as questions about them can be asked in this topic. The issues are not discussed here as they are found elsewhere in this guide (page 21).

Issues around laboratory experiments as a research method relate to laboratory experiments using animals, but other issues apply too: practical issues and ethical issues (which are considered separately).

> **Exam tip**
>
> Practical issues when using animals in laboratory experiments can be about ethics, such as using a species that might be endangered (morally they cannot be used in the same way as non-endangered species). However, there are other practical issues (e.g. handling the animals). If asked about practical issues, stick to them and do not bring ethics in, and vice versa.

Some animal studies in your course

- Pavlov used dogs in his study of classical conditioning.
- Skinner used pigeons and rats in his study of operant conditioning.
- Van den Oever et al. (one of the contemporary studies in biological psychology) used rats to look at the effects of cues on heroin relapse.

Differences in animal experiments in the laboratory compared with experiments using humans

- Animals have to be fed and housed, looked after and handled in ways that humans do not. There are practical issues involved in using animals in laboratory experiments.
- Animals are not suitable in experiments where the researchers need to know about thinking, attitudes or memory, and other such topics.
- Animals can only act and react in certain ways, so might not be suitable at all for some studies, and some species might be more suitable for some studies than others. Their size can be important or their capabilities. Their brain structure might have to be suitable.
- In general animal experiments can involve more control than laboratory experiments using humans. For example, researchers tend to make animals hungry for operant conditioning studies — hunger is not so easy to control in humans.

Strengths	Weaknesses
Animals are relatively small and usually easy to handle so procedures can be more feasible than if using humans	The brains of animals are not exactly the same as humans so generalising findings to humans might not be valuable
Some animals have short gestation periods and reproductive cycles so generations and genes can be studied more easily than with humans	Using animals in studies and then drawing conclusions about humans does not address the complexity of human processing and behaviour
Some animals have similar brain structure (e.g. rats and mice) to humans and so there is value in using animals in studies and relating the findings to humans	

Table 36 Strengths and weaknesses of using animals in experiments (non-ethical)

> **Exam tip**
>
> Be ready to include studies that have used animal experiments to illustrate your answers about animals being used in laboratory experiments.

> **Knowledge check 24**
>
> Give two practical reasons for using animals and not humans in laboratory experiments and two practical reasons for not using them instead of humans (in laboratory studies).

Ethical issues regarding the use of animals in laboratory experiments

There are special **ethical** principles for using animals in laboratory experiments. These come from the Animals (Scientific Procedures) Act (1986) and there are Home Office regulations. The British Psychological Society (BPS) has published Guidelines for Working with Animals (2012) based on the Animals (Scientific Procedures) Act (1986).

> **Exam tip**
>
> It may seem that issues like not having the right to withdraw or being able to give informed consent should apply to animals, and many would perhaps sympathise with that view. However, ethical guidelines and principles that apply to human participants should not be used when discussing the ethics of using animals in research.

A general ethical requirement when using animals is to cause the least possible distress. The BPS guidelines use these headings: legal requirements; replacing the use of animals; choice of species and strain; number of animals; procedures; procurement of animals; animal care; disposing of animals; animals in psychology teaching; the use of animals for therapeutic purposes; clinical assessment and treatment of animal behaviour. The list shows what the focus is. The requirement is to replace the use of animals where possible with non-sentient alternatives (sentient = feeling), to reduce the number of animals used and to refine procedures to give the least impact.

How to decide whether a study is 'ethical'?

Pro-animal use:

- Bateson's decision cube is useful — decisions about carrying out a study using animals have to take into account three issues: how useful the findings are going to be, what distress will be caused and how sound the research is (e.g. in terms of reliability).
- Gray (1991) argued that we have a moral responsibility to our own species to understand as much as we can, which is on the side of using animals.
- Singer (1975) argues that research should take place if for the greatest good of the greater number.
- Darwin showed through his ideas about evolution that findings from animals can be generalisable to humans.

Anti-animal use:

- Animal rights campaigners might say no animals should be used.
- Singer (1975) argues that we should not carry out on animals studies we would not do on ourselves and this is **speciesism**, like racism.
- Findings from animals might not be generalisable to humans so there is no justification for doing studies using animals.
- The cost-benefit argument does not work as the cost to the animals might not be known at the start and neither might the benefits of the findings.

Strengths	Weaknesses
Gray (1991) puts forward the 'moral obligation' view that we owe it to our own species to find out all we can and using animals can serve that purpose	There are guidelines to avoid discomfort and to protect animals, but many animals do feel pain, nonetheless
There is some benefit to animals of doing experiments using animals, such as understanding about their needs and care, which gives some ethical justification	Perhaps we have an obligation to treat animals well. This is the opposite of the '**pro-speciesism**' view

Table 37 Strengths and weaknesses in the ethics of using animals in experiments

Knowledge check 25

Outline ethical reasons for using animals in laboratory research. Make sure you avoid using human ethical guidelines and avoid using practical reasons.

Analysis of data

You need to look at inferential statistics as a way of analysing data including issues in such testing: levels of measurement, reasons for choosing a Chi-squared test, comparing observed and critical values, and levels of significance, as well as doing the Chi-squared test. You also need to look at analysis of qualitative data, using thematic analysis.

Inferential statistics

'Inferential statistics' is the overall term for the four tests in your course — used to see if the results of studies and of your practical investigations are significant or not.

Once you have gathered your data in any psychology study you need to analyse the results. You do that using descriptive statistics — mean, median, mode, range, standard deviation and graphs. You then use statistical tests to see if your results were significant or not. This section covers the information you need about inferential testing, whichever approach that requirement is listed under in your course. The coverage here is brief and was also included in *Edexcel Psychology: Social psychology and cognitive psychology (with issues and debates) Student Guide*.

The four inferential tests in your course

The four **inferential tests** you need to know about are the Spearman, Mann–Whitney U, Wilcoxon and Chi-squared tests. Table 38 shows which test is used in which circumstances. Use the table to give reasons for using the test as well as to find out which test to use.

Test of difference			
	Nominal data	Ordinal data (or interval data)	Interval data
Repeated measures or matched pairs	*Not required for your course*	Wilcoxon	*Not required for your course*
Independent groups	Chi-squared	Mann–Whitney U	*Not required for your course*
Correlation			
Ordinal data (or interval data)		Interval data	
Spearman		*Not required for your course*	

Table 38 Which inferential test to use

Questions & Answers

Learning theories Method Q2a asks which test is required for an unseen study.

Exam tip

A-level students, make sure that you can choose a test for a study, and that you can give reasons for your choice. Learn the brief summary given here as it has the information that you need. It is probably worth learning the information off by heart if you find it hard to work out.

Choosing a level of significance

You have to test how far results are likely to be due to chance. Three **levels of significance** are summarised here to remind you what a level of significance is.

If you accept that 5% of the results or fewer are due to chance, you would usually say the study 'worked' at the 5% level of significance. How you say this is $p \leq 0.05$. This means that the probability of the results being due to chance (p) is equal to or less than ($\leq$) 5% (0.05). Since 5% is 1 in 20, you would accept that 1 in 20 of the results is due to chance, while 19 in 20 (95%) are due to what was done in the study.

- 0.10 is 10% being due to chance — not acceptable
- 0.05 is 5% being due to chance — acceptable
- 0.01 is 1% being due to chance — better and more acceptable

Questions & Answers

Learning theories Method Q2d asks about level of significance and looking at whether a study is significant or not.

Levels of measurement

For your course in psychology, there are three **levels of measurement**: nominal, ordinal and interval/ratio. Check you know what these are.

(If you are doing the AS course you do not need to know about levels of measurement for the exam.)

Writing a null hypothesis

The hypothesis (the alternative, or experimental, hypothesis) is the statement of what is expected to happen in a study, and the null hypothesis states that it will not happen, because any difference or relationship will be due to chance. The null is tested by an inferential test.

Exam tip

When writing the alternative or experimental hypothesis, and the null hypothesis, make sure that both the independent variable (IV) and dependent variable (DV) are fully explained (operationalised). For example, if the IV is whether someone is driving a large or small car, say so, and do not just say 'the car they drive'.

Knowledge check 26

Give three reasons for choosing a Chi-squared test.

Exam tip

If something seems complicated, write it out in your own words three times as that can help to clarify it.

Knowledge check 27

What does it mean to say the result of a test (e.g. the Chi-squared) is significant at $p \leq 0.01$?

Exam tip

Note from Table 38 what you need to know to choose a test — levels of measurement is one of the features of data in a study that you need.

Knowledge check 28

If data are whether people are male and female and whether they can do a test or not, what type of data are they?

Knowledge check 29

Write out the null hypothesis for a study that suggests that in a department store more men will go up to the large screen televisions (over 36 inch) than women. Also say what the IV and DV are in this hypothesis.

One- or two-tailed regarding testing

- A hypothesis is directional if it says which way the results will go, for example: 'Males will drive large cars and females will drive small cars.' In testing, directional is called '**one-tailed**'.
- A hypothesis is non-directional if it does not specify which way the result will go, for example: 'There is a difference in size of car driven depending on whether the driver is male or female.' In testing, non-directional is called '**two-tailed**'.

Critical and observed values

The result of doing an inferential test is the observed value. For each type of inferential test there are tables of **critical values**, against which you can check your **observed value** to see if your result is significant.

How to compare critical and observed values

AS students do not need to know about comparing critical and observed values to judge significance for the exam.

- The observed value comes from working out the test result. The different tests have different statistics to look up, such as the T statistic for Wilcoxon.
- Then you need the right critical values table. These tables are found in statistics books or on the internet, at the front of your exam papers and in your specification. Find the right table for each test.
- Then you need to know: for the Spearman test, the number of participants (**N**); for the Mann–Whitney U-test, the number of participants in each group (this will have been an independent groups design); for the Wilcoxon test, the number of participants (N) ignoring those with 0 differences; for the Chi-squared test, the **degrees of freedom** (df), which for a 2 by 2 table is 1.
- Finally, choose a level of significance of 0.05 (5%) and decide whether your hypothesis is one- or two-tailed.
- Armed with all this information, you will be able to look along the rows and columns of the table and compare your observed value with the critical value to see if the result is significant or not.
- The table will tell you whether your result has to be larger or smaller than the one in the appropriate box of the table.

Qualitative data analysis: thematic analysis

Qualitative data are in the form of words or pictures — they are not numerical. They are normally analysed by looking for common themes in the data, not unlike doing content analysis (page 50). In **thematic analysis** themes are found and then coding is used to group data into those themes, to make the data manageable. There may be re-coding as the themes develop perhaps (themes need to be manageable, e.g. not using a theme of every idea and not using a theme that covers most of the ideas). Themes can be counted. This turns the data into quantitative data.

Exam tip

Make up some results of the three tests (e.g. ρ (rho) = 0.58, T = 2, U = 8 and Chi-squared = 4.72) and see if these results are significant, given fictitious levels of significance, numbers of participants and other features.

Thematic analysis:

- Become familiar with the data that have been gathered.
- Code the data — work through some common themes in the data.
- Define and name the themes.
- Code the data again, this time using the chosen themes (aiming not to interpret the data in the light of the research question).
- Check the themes represent the meanings of the participants.
- Throughout a **reflexive journal** can be kept by the researchers so they can refer to it when explaining their analysis process. This can help in maintaining objectivity.
- Look for reliability and validity in the themes.
- Report the results.

Strengths	Weaknesses
It is a way of reducing data to a manageable size so that they can be summarised and the validity is maintained if the analysis is done well	Even though there can be good validity, it can be hard to judge the validity if the way the themes were developed is not fully explained
Validity is good because themes come from the data and not from the researcher or the research question, which reduces bias	The analysis takes time because there are a lot of data to be analysed and the coder has to be familiar with the data. It also requires skill

Table 39 Strengths and weaknesses of using thematic analysis to analyse qualitative data

Scientific status of psychology

One of the issues and debates in your course is about psychology being a science. This issue is important enough in method in psychology for it to feature in learning theories as a separate section.

Your course has a list of issues that relate to psychology and science, and they are listed here to help your revision:

- **Replicability**: this means a study can be done again (repeated) to see if the same results are found. To be replicable a study usually needs careful controls, such as standardised instructions. Science needs to see if results are reliable, so studies must be replicable.
- **Reliability**: this means when a study is done again the same results are found. Science needs to have reliable findings, where they occur over and over again, and can predict what will happen in a given situation.
- **Validity**: this means that data represent real life and represent what it is claimed they represent. Data that are not valid are not much use when studying human behaviour — it would not be 'human behaviour' that was being studied.
- **Internal validity**: this means that any cause-and-effect conclusion drawn from a study is acceptable, in that there is no bias that might affect such a conclusion, and no other 'cause'. As there is not likely to be no bias, it is the degree of internal validity that is important — a study needs as much as possible.
- **Predictive validity**: this means that a score predicts what it is claiming to predict. If a test for a job application has predictive validity, then a later test of the applicant (how well they are doing the job perhaps) should show that the application test had validity.
- **Ecological validity**: this means that the results represent what it is claimed they represent in terms of the situation and setting they are in — in terms of their ecology. Data that are not valid are not useful.

Exam tip

Be ready to answer a question about analysis of qualitative data in as much detail as you would discuss analysis of quantitative data.

Knowledge check 30

If an observer made a note that a child was standing alone in the playground and not mixing with other children, also when another child approached them they turned away and walked to another area in the playground, as well as not watching other children playing, what theme or themes might emerge from the data?

- **Reductionism**: this means the way science looks at parts of a whole, in order to use controls and study something systematically. This focus can mean reducing behaviour to something not 'real' and not 'whole'. Science needs to draw cause-and-effect conclusions and must often reduce what is to be studied to something manageable.
- **Falsification**: this means looking at a claim (hypothesis) to see if it can be shown not to be the case. For example, we can find helpful females many times but we cannot say all females are helpful. When we find one unhelpful female we can show the opposite is the case (not all females are helpful) — we can falsify but not prove.
- **Empiricism**: this is the idea that knowledge comes only from sense data. Empirical data are data collected by sight, sound, taste, smell and touch — through our senses. Science uses empirical data to test hypotheses that are derived from theories.
- **Hypothesis testing**: this is within the scientific method. A theory is generated, hypotheses are derived from the theory, empirical testing takes place and then the theory is either accepted, rejected or amended in the light of the data.
- **Use of controls**: science requires firm data that are reliable and objective. Science tends to use methods like experiments as they are more likely to give reliable, objective data. To draw firm conclusions studies need to use controls carefully, to avoid bias.

Is psychology a science?

Some psychology is more scientific than other psychology:

- Biological psychology uses scientific methods like scanning and experiments.
- Learning theories use experiments, such as Pavlov's and Skinner's experiments with animals and Bandura's work with children.
- Content analysis might be less scientific in that the key terms that are counted, for example, are chosen by the researcher. Nevertheless counting key terms is a replicable method and reliability can be shown, so that is scientific.
- Research with animals in laboratory experiments is done scientifically, sometimes using careful lesioning, for example, to track down what a particular brain area is for.
- Observations might be less scientific as they can be naturalistic, done in someone's own environment, and so affected perhaps by situational variables like time of day.
- Observations using tallying and obtaining inter-observer reliability might be seen as more scientific.
- Some subject matter is perhaps more scientific. Science can be seen in biological psychology, in its subject matter (e.g. genes, hormones, the central nervous system and neurotransmitter functioning).
- Cognitive psychology looks at brain structures and their role in information processing in the brain which moves into neuroscience.
- Social psychology uses experiments and controls, such as Milgram's work, although it also uses questionnaires and interviews to find out about attitudes to others, which is less scientific.

Exam tip

Use the terms in this section to write a paragraph about what science is and how psychology fits as a science. Be sure to explain any terms you use in answers so that you show knowledge with understanding (which is what gets marks).

Questions & Answers

Biological psychology Content Q3 considers whether the psychodynamic approach is unscientific, which can be useful in the debate about psychology and science.

Summary

- There are different types of observation — two main types (naturalistic and structured) and four other types (covert, overt, participant, non-participant).
- The different types of observation have different strengths and weaknesses focusing on issues such as objectivity–subjectivity and validity. For example, participant observations may not be as objective as non-participant ones because the person is both participant in the process and observer. Also, covert observations may not be as ethical as overt ones as the participants cannot be contacted directly beforehand.
- Naturalistic observations are done in the participants' natural setting and structured observations involve setting up a situation, so are less natural.
- Content analysis is a useful method for looking at documents, drawings, artefacts and written material.
- The methodology for the learning approach also involves reviewing your learning about laboratory experiments in particular when using animals, and being able to describe and evaluate the use of animals in laboratory experiments.
- Ethical issues when using animals in laboratory experiments are also required in this section, including the Animals (Scientific Procedures) Act (1986) and Home Office Regulations.

- Material about inferential testing that is given in this section also includes material for biological psychology: it is about the three types of hypothesis, one- or two-tailed regarding tests, levels of significance, critical and observed values, and levels of measurement. One-tailed testing is for when a direction for the results is predicted in the hypothesis. Levels of significance that are acceptable are 0.01 and 0.05. Levels of measurement are nominal, ordinal and interval/ratio.
- Spearman is the test for correlations, in biological psychology, and Chi-squared is the test used in learning theories.
- Material about inferential testing other than that listed in the two bullet points above involves the reasons for choosing the tests (focusing on the four tests which are Spearman's, Mann–Whitney U, Wilcoxon and Chi-squared) and focus on how to compare the observed (found) value with the critical value (the value that the tables predict).
- The scientific status of psychology, including many issues that relate to that discussion, is covered. Issues include replicability, reliability, validity (internal, predictive and ecological), reductionism, falsification, empiricism, hypothesis testing and the use of controls.

Studies

Classic study: Watson and Rayner (1920)

Watson and Rayner (1920) carried out a study using classical conditioning to see if they could cause a fear in a human baby they called 'Little Albert'. Use a textbook or some other source to remind yourself about the aims and procedure of this study.

Questions & Answers

Learning theories Studies Q1 asks about the aims of the Little Albert study.

Results and conclusions

- The results of the study were that Little Albert did become conditioned to fear his pet rat. When he heard the loud noise that had been used to instil fear in him he was afraid. Quite soon he associated the pet rat with the loud noise and showed fear even without the noise present. He had learned a fear through classical conditioning principles.

- At 11 months 10 days old he started to cry as soon as he saw the rat, even without the noise, after the pairings. Little Albert transferred his fear to a rabbit and partly to cotton wool and a fur coat. This was taken to show generalisation of the fear from the pet rat to other furry things (11 months 15 days). The researchers also used a different setting and the fear transferred to the new setting as well, though the fear response seemed less intense (11 months 20 days).
- The researchers concluded that the fear was transferred to different stimuli and to a different situation.
- The researchers did have to reintroduce the pairing of the noise and the rat as the association did weaken during the study.

Strengths	Weaknesses
The experiment was well-designed and controlled, e.g. the independent variable each time was clear and the dependent variable (the behaviour) was measured and recorded carefully	It was not ethical because Albert was distressed throughout and even though he was distressed the study continued for weeks
The study showed that Pavlov's ideas about classical conditioning (from his work with dogs) could be said to be true of humans	The setting was a laboratory and, therefore, artificial; the study lacked ecological validity and perhaps validity with regard to the task

Table 40 Strengths and weaknesses of Watson and Rayner (1920)

Contemporary study: Becker et al. (2002)

You have three contemporary studies to choose from. They are Becker et al. (2002), Bastian et al. (2011) and Capafóns et al. (1998). Becker et al. (2002) is summarised here. However, if you have studied one of the other two you might prefer to revise your own chosen study instead. Your textbook will give your more detail.

Becker et al. (2002) suits the key question that is used here, so you might find it useful anyway.

Aims

Television was about to be introduced into the Fijian culture. The culture had no previous media influence. The aim was to study the effects of television on eating disorders. Becker et al. (2002) mention eating disorders are more common in industrialised countries, which suggests a role for culture and their aim is to see if culture is a 'cause' for eating disorders.

Questions & Answers

Learning theories Studies Q1 asks about the aims of Becker et al. (2002).

Procedure

The study used 63 girls (average age about 17 years) in 1995 within a few weeks of television being introduced and then another group of 65 girls (also in the school) in 1998, 3 years after television had arrived in the area. Qualitative data were gathered

Exam tip

Little Albert was taken away from the study so the fear was not 'put right' as far as is known. However, little is known about who Little Albert was, so it is hard to make claims about what happened after the study. There is still argument about his true identity. Also the researchers did find the association wore off over time.

Knowledge check 31

Explain two weaknesses of the Little Albert study (1920).

in the form of stories about feelings and behaviour related to the introduction of television. The EAT-26 questionnaire was used (26 items about eating attitudes — a score of 20 was high). A semi-structured interview was also used (open-ended questions getting qualitative data from 30 of the girls in the sample, chosen because they showed disordered eating attitudes and television viewing habits). In the study questions were about body image and dieting, as well as about television viewing habits in the household.

Results and conclusions

Becker et al. (2002) used a Chi-squared test to look for significant differences in the quantitative data (attitudes to eating and diet before and after television) and thematic analysis to get ideas from the qualitative data.

- 41.3% of the 1995 sample said their household had a television compared with 70.8% in 1998, which confirmed the likely growth in television watching over the period. This was a significant difference, found using the Chi-squared test ($p \leq 0.001$).
- 12.7% in 1995, compared with 29.2% (more than double) in 1998, had a score on the EAT-26 questionnaire of more than 20.
- 0% said they used self-induced vomiting to control weight in 1995 compared with 11.3% in 1998.
- There was an association between television ownership and changed dieting behaviour but not enough evidence to show television *watching* had caused the change. Girls in a household with television were 3 times as likely to have an EAT-26 score of over 20.
- The qualitative data showed a desire to be like television characters in terms of clothing, hairstyle and body reshaping.

Strengths	Weaknesses
The use of qualitative data added depth and detail to the findings as it was in the qualitative data that links between what was watched and eating behaviour were confirmed	The study used an independent groups design so there may have been participant variables that gave the differences in findings between the 1995 and 1998 samples
There were careful controls such as the use of the same questionnaire, so findings could be compared between the two samples	The choice of such a specific culture with regard to eating habits means that generalisation of the findings to other cultures might not be possible

Table 41 Strengths and weaknesses of Becker et al. (2002)

Summary

- For learning theories, as with other topic areas in your course, you have to cover one classic study and one contemporary study from a choice of three.
- The classic study in learning theories is Watson and Rayner's (1920) study of Little Albert, when they conditioned a fear response in a small child.
- For the contemporary study in learning theories you can choose Becker et al. (2002) who looked at eating behaviours in adolescent girls in Fiji when television was first introduced and again after it had been introduced for some time.
- Or you can choose to study Bastian et al. (2011) who looked at how playing a violent video game affects people's views of their humanity.
- Or you can choose to study Capafóns et al. (1998) who looked at the effectiveness of systematic desensitisation in helping with a fear of flying.

Exam tip

Becker et al. (2002) is a useful example of a study using a questionnaire, and also using semi-structured interviewing, so you can use it when discussing those methods. It is also a 'before and after' study (before television and after television), which can be useful when discussing method.

Exam tip

Becker et al. (2002) can be used as an example of use of the Chi-squared test and of thematic analysis, both of which feature in the Method section of learning theories in your course.

Knowledge check 32

List three results from Becker et al.'s (2002) study.

Key question

You need to know about one key question which concepts and research in learning theories can explain. The question must be important to today's society. One key question is looked at in this book. However, you may have studied a different one and might prefer to revise it instead.

Is the influence of role models and celebrities something that causes anorexia?

Describing the question

A common accusation is that thin role models are linked to increasing diagnoses of anorexia, particularly perhaps in girls, but also in boys. The issue is whether such models do cause eating disorders or whether there is another explanation. Sufferers of anorexia regard themselves as fat even when they are dangerously underweight (weight at least 15% lower than it should be). There is a high incidence of anorexia among teenage girls and the rate of anorexia in boys is rising.

Concepts, theories and research from learning theories in your course

Explaining the influence of role models on the development of anorexia using theories, concepts and studies from learning theories

Social learning theory suggests that people imitate role models, especially those they see as relevant to themselves. Teenagers may imitate female models and media celebrities, where there is a trend to be very slim/thin. There are also rewards for being thin through praise and admiration from friends and family. And there is negative reinforcement against being fat, because being fat brings criticism and teasing.

However, anorexia could also be explained in a different way. The psychodynamic approach suggests that a girl might starve herself to avoid growing up because she is fixated at a certain psychosexual stage. Nevertheless, cross-cultural studies support the idea of anorexia being learned, because the incidence of anorexia differs in different cultures according to varying social norms.

There is evidence for social learning linking to anorexia nervosa. Becker et al. (2002) found that having a television in the household linked to more focus on weight and dieting in girls about 17 years old in Fiji — 0% in 1995, just as television was being introduced said they used self-induced vomiting to control weight compared with 11.3% in 1998, 3 years after television was introduced. Becker et al. (2002) felt they found enough evidence to link the arrival of the television with an increased focus on cultural values around dieting and weight. This supports the social learning view that cultural attitudes can be learned through observational learning and imitating role models.

> **Exam tip**
>
> Note that most of an answer relating a topic area (here, learning theories) to explain a key issue should be about that topic area. However, it is worth making one point about an alternative explanation in evaluation. It is also worth giving evidence, such as using Bandura et al. (1961, 1963 and 1965) as evidence for modelling and imitation.

> **Exam tip**
>
> It is important to describe the issue itself, such as why it is a problem for society or the individual. Here it is not just 'anorexia' that is the issue, but whether it is caused by role models, in which case such modelling should be stopped.

> **Knowledge check 33**
>
> Using the key question of anorexia and socially learned behaviour, list four points you can build on to give a learning theory explanation for the issue.

Questions & Answers

Learning theories Key question Q1 considers the key question of role models influencing the prevalence of anorexia nervosa.

Summary

- One key question is whether anorexia nervosa is caused by thin role models on television.
- Role models have been very thin, with size 0 models being used, even though there has been focus for a little while on having more 'normal' models. Photographs are air-brushed to make models look better.
- Those with anorexia nervosa do think they look fat when they are not, which suggests an aspect of their thinking being a cause.
- Becker et al. (2002) found a link in Fijian girls between the arrival of television and the focus on diet and weight. This is evidence that role models can affect attitudes and behaviour.
- Observational learning suggests we imitate role models, which would back the idea of role models on television being copied, including their thinness.
- Celebrities seem to be rewarded for their looks, such as being praised, which fits with social learning too, as it suggests vicarious reinforcement happens, when we imitate behaviour we have seen rewarded.

Practical investigation

You will have carried out a practical within learning theories, using one or more observations. Go back over your notes to revise what you did, as it is not possible here to help you to revise that part of the course.

Questions & Answers

Learning theories Practical investigation Q1 asks about your practical investigation and gives suggested answers to help your learning.

Some general ideas about the practical and what to learn

- Ensure that your observation(s) relate to learned behaviour.
- You need to have gathered both qualitative and quantitative data in one or more observations, and to have included tallying, note taking and thematic analysis.

Questions & Answers

Learning theories Practical investigation Q1a asks about how you gathered your quantitative data.

- Be ready to explain whether your observation was covert, overt, participant or non-participant, structured or naturalistic.
- Make sure you know about controls you put in place and why (as relevant). Also think about what was not controlled, and the reasons for this.

- Make sure you know about ethical issues you dealt with, and perhaps also some ethical issues you could not address and the reason for this.
- Note your reasons for choosing a Chi-squared test, the level of significance, the level of measurement, that it was an independent groups design, and whether the test had to be one-or two-tailed (and why). Note whether the result of the test (the observed value) was significant or not by checking against the critical values (see page 55 for explanations of this).
- Write up the results and analysis of results (e.g. descriptive statistics as appropriate as well as the Chi-squared).
- Write up the results of the qualitative analysis and your use of thematic analysis.
- Be ready to evaluate your study in terms of validity, reliability, generalisability and credibility.

Exam tip

Practise using these bullet points as questions and prepare answers. For example, 'What controls did you put in place and why?' Use past papers to see what sort of questions are asked about practical investigations (you can use GCE 2008 as well as the specimen materials for GCE 2015).

Questions & Answers

Learning theories Practical investigation Q1b asks about the credibility of your study (giving examples).

Knowledge check 34

What was the result of the test you carried out for your practical? What was the critical value you had to match or exceed? Was your result significant or not — and if so, at what level?

Summary

- You will have carried out an observation to look for differences and the observation will have involved an independent groups design.
- You will have collected quantitative data that will have allowed a Chi-squared test (so it will be nominal data).
- You will have adhered to ethical principles, so be sure you know how you did this and what issues there were.
- You will have done the test, found the result, looked at the critical value you had to match or exceed, and decided whether your result was significant or not and at what level.

- You will have drawn conclusions and been able to evaluate your results using issues of validity, reliability, generalisability and credibility.
- You will have carried out an observation and gathered qualitative data (might be all one observation that gathered both qualitative and quantitative data) and will have used thematic analysis to analyse the qualitative data.
- You will have written up the results section of a report, including both the quantitative and qualitative data findings and including appropriate graphs and tables as well as the thematic analysis.

Exam tip

Turn these bullet points into questions and answer them, as you are likely to be asked about them. For example: 'Outline the aim of your practical and state the hypothesis for 2 marks each, and consider two ethical issues you addressed.'

Exam tip

You might be asked to plan a practical based on a short scenario. Use your understanding of methodology from your own practical to devise a different one.

Issues and debates (A-level only)

If you are studying for the AS, you do not need to know about issues and debates.

To help A-level students to become familiar with the 11 'issues and debates' ready for their Topic 9 section, they are explained at the end of each topic area. They are reviewed here with social psychology in mind.

Issue and debate in psychology	Links to learning theories in your course
Ethical issues in research	Ethics are important in psychology, including when using animals in laboratory experiments. The Animals (Scientific Procedures) Act (1986) is used to protect animals and there are ethical principles when using animals such as about their caging, their care and minimising their distress.
Practical issues in research	Observations bring practical issues such as how to record data if the observation is an overt one. Also structured observations are used partly because of practical reasons. Some situations are found so infrequently they need to be set up. Animal research also has practical issues, such as obtaining the animals and achieving results that can be said to be true for humans.
Reductionism	Animal studies reduce what is being studied to a small piece of, for example, brain functioning. For example, looking to see how drugs work in the brains of animals necessarily avoids issues of peer pressure in drug taking.
Explaining using different themes	The two theories of conditioning and social learning theory look at how behaviour is learned using different themes, such as stimulus-response learning as opposed to learning by observation.
Psychology as a science	Conditioning theories come from experiments, and controls are used to isolate the IV and DV. This is doing scientific method. Observations can be less scientific, if, for example, they are naturalistic.
Cultural and gender issues in research	Operant conditioning theory would suggest that both cultural issues and gender behaviour are learned through reinforcement principles. Social learning theory suggests that both are learned through observing others.
Nature–nurture	Skinner's work on operant conditioning reduced behaviour to nurture, suggesting that we learn through being rewarded or punished and through reinforcement schedules, for example. Behaviourists removed the issue of nature by focusing on the measurable and the observable.
Development over time	Treatments using behaviourism have changed over time, from using flooding as a technique to help with phobias, through to now perhaps still using systematic desensitisation ideas but often with some element of cognitive-behavioural therapy (CBT) too.
Social control	Classical conditioning can be linked to social control in that advertising uses such principles to shape behaviour. Operant conditioning has led to therapies such as token economy where someone is rewarded for required behaviour. Society or its representatives (e.g. in prison) decide what behaviour is required and this can be seen as a form of social control. If we copy what we see and what we see rewarded (vicarious reinforcement) then television and video games perhaps need to be monitored, but any such monitoring can be seen as social control.
Use of psychology within society	Knowing how learning comes through either classical conditioning, a pattern of rewards or copying the behaviour of others can be a help to society — such as instigating the 9 p.m. watershed to protect children from what they might see and imitate (e.g. violence).
Socially sensitive research	Therapies all tend to have a therapist who has power in the situation. Even those who aim not to have this power relationship have it because the client tends to see the therapist as having the power. This is a socially sensitive area of research, because it implies that a client is less able to cope in society. Skinner's ideas about learning by reinforcement are socially sensitive if they are taken as explaining all learning — school learning using rewards could be seen as society using brainwashing, for example.

Table 42 Issues and debates and how learning theories illustrate each

Questions & Answers

Learning theories Issues and debates Q1 asks about how psychology has developed over time (drawing on learning theories and biological psychology).

Exam tip

The 11 issues and debates are repeated at the end of each topic area to show how that topic area illustrates them. You could make notes for each issue and debate, drawing together all the ideas in the topic areas, so that you have a wide range of examples of that issue/debate.

Summary: learning theories

- There are three main learning theories: classical conditioning; operant conditioning; and social learning theory. The three theories have different terms and features.
- Pavlov (1927) and three of Bandura's studies (1961, 1963, 1965) are covered.
- The focus is also on how learning theories explain the acquisition and maintenance of phobias and treatments for phobias based on learning theories, including systematic desensitisation.
- Individual differences are looked at when considering different reinforcement patterns engendering different behaviours in individuals and different role model imitating also giving different learning and behaviour.
- Development is considered by looking at the three learning theories too, because they all have ideas about how we develop: classical conditioning through associations between stimuli and responses; operant conditioning through patterns of rewards and punishments;

- social learning through watching others and imitating their behaviour.
- Methods covered in learning theories include observation and content analysis. Both qualitative and quantitative data are considered. Another method is the use of animals in laboratory experiments, with a focus on related ethical issues. Analysis of quantitative data focuses on inferential statistics and related issues, with the test being Chi-squared. Analysis of qualitative data is by thematic analysis.
- The methods section also includes a focus on psychology and science.
- The classic study is Watson and Rayner (1920) and the chosen contemporary study is Becker et al. (2002).
- The chosen key question is: 'Is the influence of role models and celebrities something that causes anorexia?'
- There is a practical investigation which must be an observation and gather both qualitative and quantitative data.

Questions & Answers

The section follows the structure of the course, with biological psychology first and then learning theories. The questions follow the course structure within each area too:

- overview of the topic
- content
- method
- studies
- key question
- practical
- issues and debates (A-level only)

Unless otherwise stated, the example questions can be used as practice questions for both AS Paper 2 and A-level Paper 1 — and for the methods sections and the issues and debates section, A-level Paper 3 too, as indicated.

The difference between the AS and A-level papers is that there will be more marks awarded for AO1 at AS. There will also be no issues and debates at AS.

Examination issues

Assessment objectives

You are marked according to assessment objectives (AOs). You can find these in the specification, but they are summarised here:

- **AO1** — knowledge with understanding of scientific ideas, processes, techniques and procedures (knowing and understanding)
- **AO2** — applying knowledge and understanding of scientific ideas, processes, techniques and procedures (applying)
- **AO3** — analysing, interpreting and evaluating a range of scientific information, ideas and evidence to make judgements and reach conclusions and also to refine practical design and procedures (commenting)

A good plan is to consider the exam paper as covering the three AOs in equal proportions (one third each) and to consider the four topic areas and sections within them to be covered evenly. That will help you when preparing.

Exam questions and marking

For both AS and A-level, your exams will have some points-based marking and some levels-based marking:

- up to 8 marks is likely to mean points-based, which means 1 mark for each point clearly made
- 8 marks and over is likely to be levels marking, which means a mark depending on where in bands the answer fits

AS Papers 1 and 2: expect short-answer questions that are points-based and some extended writing, some with 8 marks and one with 12 marks (though not focusing on issues and debates).

A-level Paper 1: expect short-answer questions that are points-based. Also some 8-mark questions and at the end a 12-mark question on issues and debates.

A-level Paper 3: some of the short-answer method questions can suit A-level Paper 3, as can some of the questions on studies and issues and debates. Where a question in this guide suits Paper 3 that is noted.

Extended open-response questions: allocation of AOs

The different mark allocations for extended open-response questions have different assessment objective splits. Extended open-response questions are from 8 marks:

- 8 marks can be split into: AO1 4 marks and AO2* 4 marks; or AO1 4 marks and AO3 4 marks
- 12 marks can be split into: AO1 4 marks, AO2* 4 marks and AO3 4 marks; or AO1 6 marks, AO3 6 marks
- 16 marks can be split into: AO1 6 marks, AO2* 4 marks and AO3 6 marks; or AO1 6 marks and AO3 10 marks
- 20 marks can be split into: AO1 8 marks, AO2* 4 marks and AO3 8 marks; or AO1 8 marks and AO3 12 marks

*You will know if you need to focus on AO2 (applying your knowledge and understanding) because there will be a scenario to apply it to and a comment about you needing to refer to the scenario. Without a scenario to apply your knowledge and understanding to, the marks will be AO1 and AO3 with the splits as outlined here.

How to use this section

- Choose one topic area and revise the material using this guide. Work through the questions for your chosen topic area, answering them yourself before reading the advice on how to answer the question or reading the answer given.
- Then read through the advice on what is required and mark your own answers. Did you interpret the question successfully? Read through the answers given and note where the marks were awarded. Finally, read through the comments to see what a full answer should include.
- Once you have prepared answers for all the questions in a particular approach, answer them again choosing a different topic. For example, if you described one theory of learning within the learning approach, describe another theory of learning. In this way you are making up your own questions, which is useful preparation for the examination.
- Specimen questions can be found on the Edexcel website (www.edexcel.com), together with mark schemes. When you think you have revised enough, try to answer them.

Exam commentary

All questions and answers are followed by exam commentary. These are preceded by the icon **e** or **e**. They indicate what a question requires, where credit is due, strengths in the answer, areas for improvement, specific problems, common errors, lack of clarity, irrelevance, mistakes in the meaning of terms and/or misinterpretation of the question. The comments also indicate how the answers might be marked in an exam — there are ticks in the answers to show where exactly marks could be awarded.

■ Biological psychology

Overview

(1) Describe what is meant by biological psychology. (3 marks)

e There are 3 points-based AO1 marks. There is 1 mark for each point that focuses on what biological psychology is.

Student answer

Biological psychology focuses on human biology, the parts that relate to the functioning of the brain for the most part. There is focus on the central nervous system, which is the brain and the spinal column. ✓ Some psychology focuses on the autonomic nervous system, which governs some responses such as the flight-or-fight response. The brain is hard to study as a whole and focus in biological psychology is on functioning at the synapse where neurotransmitters send message and where drugs work. ✓ Focus is also on brain structures and what they are 'for', such as the amygdala, a structure that relates to aggression. ✓ In fact, biological psychology also focuses on animals and their amygdala also relates to aggression, for example, showing that animal brain functioning has quite a bit in common with human brain functioning. (✓) The idea of survival of the fittest is also covered in biological psychology.

e **3/3 marks awarded.** There is enough here for 4 marks as shown by the tick in brackets. There is quite a lot of information about what biological psychology includes in your course and there is clear knowledge with understanding. There is also some mention of other areas such as the autonomic nervous system. However, the answer if anything is too detailed.

Content

(1) Define four terms that are used when describing how neurotransmitters work in the brain and for each briefly explain their part in the process. (4 marks)

e There are 4 points-based AO1 marks. There is 1 mark for each definition.

Student answer

The *synapse* is the gap between the terminal buttons of one neuron and the dendrites of another neuron. ✓ The *receptors* are at the dendrites and receive the neurotransmitter if there is a fit and if they are not already 'filled'. ✓ The *neuron* is the term for the cell body, axon, terminal buttons and dendrites — it is the whole section that takes up the neurotransmitter. ✓ An *electrical impulse*, coming from the cell body after it receives the neurotransmitter from the receptors, is sent down the axon, and the impulse causes the release of the neurotransmitter and the process continues. ✓

ⓔ **4/4 marks awarded.** The four terms are synapse, receptors, neuron and impulse, though axon, dendrites and cell body are also mentioned and could get credit. All four terms are identified and it is clear what part they play in the process so each gets the 1 definition mark.

(2) The psychodynamic approach has been criticised as not being scientific. Science focuses on objective and measurable data. Explain why the psychodynamic approach might be said to be unscientific. (4 marks)

ⓔ There are 4 points-based AO3 marks. This question could be part of the methodology section, where science is featured in the learning theories part of your course. It is here, however, to show you that the sections are not separate in the exam and you can use information from more than one section when answering a question.

Student answer

The psychodynamic approach involves concepts such as the unconscious and the id, the part of the personality found in the unconscious. The unconscious is not something that can be measured as it is a concept not part of the brain so the approach is said to be unscientific. ✓ Specific measurable data cannot be gathered. The id too, and other parts of the personality, are not measurable, and science requires measurable empirical data to be gathered to get cause-and-effect conclusions. ✓ Also Freud had to interpret the data he gathered because what is in the unconscious has to be uncovered in ways such as interpreting symbols, which brings in an element of subjectivity. ✓ Science needs to be objective because subjective data might not be repeatable or testable. Replicability is important, to test for reliability. Findings that are not repeated if a study is done again are not useful in building a body of knowledge, which science aims to do. ✓

ⓔ **4/4 marks awarded.** There is easily enough here for 4 marks. The two areas (measurable and objective) are both addressed. Reliability is also addressed and there is mention of empirical data. There are no marks for description, but it is necessary to give some description (e.g. about the unconscious and the id) to explain the point (e.g. about the concepts not being measurable).

(3) Explain how biological psychology can relate to how people develop. (4 marks)

ⓔ There are 4 points-based AO1 marks. In your course you need to be able to talk about individual differences in people or development in people in relation to the topic areas you are studying (in this case biological psychology). This question asks about development. 'Explain' questions require some information that is then justified and linked to the question.

Student answer

The role of evolution in development is important. Each person's genome, which is their collection of genes, guides what they are and what they become, such as their gender, eye colour, temperament and other characteristics. ✓ According to the idea of survival of the fittest, genes are passed on through reproduction. Only the organism that is suited to its environment will survive to adulthood so that it can reproduce its genes, those not suited will have died out. ✓ The idea is that there will be survival of the fittest (most suited) genes and evolution will take place. This means that our development is strongly guided by our genetic inheritance. ✓ This is a nature argument, as opposed to a nurture one, which might suggest we develop through our interactions with others. Inherited characteristics might include a tendency to aggression or a certain personality type. ✓

ⓔ **4/4 marks awarded.** The ideas given in relation to development are evolution, genes, survival of the fittest and the nature argument. These get the marks. The point about nurture affecting development too is interesting and shows good knowledge and understanding but is not directly related to the question so does not get a mark on its own. The answer mentions eye colour, gender, temperament, aggression and personality as characteristics that might affect us, including our development, related to our biology, so there are a good number of examples to illustrate the points made.

Method (also A-level Paper 3)

(1) Evaluate twin studies as a research method, using one twin study.   (6 marks)

ⓔ There are 6 points-based AO3 marks. You do not have to describe twin studies here, just say what is good and bad about them. There are 6 marks, so making six points is the straightforward way to get the marks, although if you make fewer than six points but elaborate on some you can get the additional marks that way. The question focuses on one twin study as that is the requirement of your course. You can use the one study to evaluate the method. You can draw on general understanding of the twin studies method as well, to evaluate.

Student answer

Twin studies involve comparing MZ and DZ twins on the basis that MZ twins share 100% of their genes and DZ share 50% of their genes, so any difference in concordance between the two types of twin is said to be down to genes. The problem is that both sets of twins share their environment too so it is hard to say the similarities in a pair of twins are down to their genes. ✓ Identical twins (MZ) might share their environment more because, looking identical, they are treated more similarly than DZ twins, which can further affect conclusions drawn as again environment is mixed in with genes. ✓ Brendgen et al. (2005) found social aggression showed similar concordance rates for both MZ and DZ twins so perhaps they shared the social environment, being at the same school, for example. ✓ Twin studies are used to say that a characteristic is down to nature.

However, this is hard to prove even with twin studies because no characteristic appears in MZ twins 100% of the time so there must be environmental causes as well, which are hard to control for. In Brendgen et al.'s study the concordance rates were not 100%. ✓ Twin studies are reasonably valid because they involve simply looking for characteristics rather than manipulating variables, so they tend to be about real-life characteristics. Although Brendgen et al. used teacher and peer ratings to judge social and physical aggression in the twins, and this is perhaps a matter of interpretation rather than a clear measure. ✓ Brendgen et al. (2005) used DZ twins of the same gender as one issue in twin studies is that non-identical twins can differ in gender whereas MZ twins are the same gender. Brendgen et al. in this way used careful controls. ✓

ℯ 6/6 marks awarded. Although the study does not feature in all the marking points, the first two marking points are the general ones and set the scene, which is useful. The other 4 marks are given for a point either about the study or illustrated by the study. You can see that quite a bit has to be written for a mark to be awarded.

Studies

(1) Describe two of Raine et al.'s (1997) results. (2 marks)

ℯ There are 2 points-based AO1 marks. Give two results from Raine et al.'s study in reasonable detail so that you show knowledge with understanding. This is pure recall, you just need to 'describe'.

Student answer

Raine et al. (1997) found lower glucose metabolism in some of the prefrontal areas of the brain of the participants charged with murder and pleading not guilty by reason of insanity. ✓ They found, however, that there were no significant differences between the 'murderers' and the 'controls' in the temporal lobe. ✓

ℯ 2/2 marks awarded. This answer clearly gives detail about the findings. In both results the part of the brain is named and whether there was a difference or not is given. It is clear who the participants were as well, so the result is detailed in that sense.

(2) Compare the procedure of Raine et al. (1997) with the procedure of one study from Li et al. (2013), Brendgen et al. (2005) and van den Oever et al. (2008). (4 marks)

ℯ There are 4 points-based AO3 marks. You can give four separate comparison points (similarities or differences) or you can give fewer and use elaboration to get the additional marks.

Student answer

Raine et al. (1997) used PET scanning to gather information about the brains of murderers (pleading not guilty) compared with controls whereas Brendgen et al. (2005) used ratings of teachers and of peers to look at aggression in twins. These research methods are very different. ✓ PET scanning requires equipment and careful procedures, more than one person measuring the scans that are produced and the dependent variable firmly gathers quantitative data which are interval/ratio data. Brendgen et al. (2005), however, use ratings, which give ordinal data and though quantitative, are likely to involve an element of interpretation. So one difference is in the level of measurement of the data. ✓ Another difference is in the level of interpretation that might give bias in the results, though it could be argued that Raine et al. (1997) had to choose which brain areas to measure, which involved some interpretation. ✓ Both studies have the aim of looking at aggression, with Raine et al. (1997) choosing to look at people who had shown a level of violence and Brendgen et al. in their procedure choosing to gather data about social as well as physical aggression. So another difference is that whereas both studied physical aggression, one focused also on social aggression, taking a wider interpretation of aggression. Also Raine et al. looked at a level of violence that was greater than Brengen et al.'s definition of physical aggression. ✓

ⓔ 4/4 marks awarded. There is a lot of material in this answer and it takes some time for the answer to get to the differences and similarities. It would be better perhaps to give the difference/similarity first and then the justification for the point as the marker has to track back to find the justification. However, there is clearly enough here for full marks and the answer focuses on the question — it is the procedure that is compared, not other parts of the study.

Key question

(1) An article in the *Guardian* in 2014 states that one in three Britons have taken illegal drugs. In 2008 the figure was 27%, and in 2014 that figure had increased to 31%. According to the article, 87% of those who take drugs do not believe they have a problem. Many drug users break the habit, but 31% of current users have had a problem with drugs and still use them. It seems clear from these figures that drug taking is a key question for society as it affects so many of the population. The article goes on to say that 47% of the population thought that a scheme where illegal drugs were available on prescription for some addicts would be a good idea, to help to reduce crime related to drug addiction. This is not the same as using drug therapy to treat addicts, which is a legal therapy. The article figures come from online interviews of 1080 UK adults.

Discuss, using concepts, theories and/or research in biological psychology, the key question for society of how effective drug therapy is for treating addiction. You must make reference to the content in your answer. (8 marks)

ⓔ There are 8 levels-based marks here, with 4 knowledge and understanding marks (AO1) and 4 marks for applying psychology to the source/key question (AO2). Your answer must draw on biological psychology including the content and studies in your course in that topic area. 'Discuss' asks you to explore the issue, giving different viewpoints. You do not have to come to a conclusion or judgement. Page 37 of the specimen assessment A-level materials available on the Edexcel website has a levels mark scheme for an 8-mark 'Discuss' question with stimulus material, which is the mark scheme that would be used for this question.

Student answer

Drug therapy for drug addiction involves giving the addict a drug that will mimic the drug of choice without giving the side effects or addiction properties of that drug — as far as that is possible. The idea is that the person is still taking a drug that has some of the properties of their drug of choice to prevent cravings and/or withdrawal symptoms, but does not have other issues to deal with, such as the addiction and side effects. Buprenorphine is a substitute for heroin. It is an opioid and produces euphoria, as heroin would. However, it can be taken in low doses and does not have the same effect as heroin or methadone (which is another drug that has been used in therapy as a substitute for heroin). Buprenorphine does not have side effects like breathing difficulties, which other opiates do and it is safer. It is the neurotransmitter functioning at the synapse which mimics heroin, which Buprenorphine will do because it is an opiate like heroin. Methadone can be more effective if someone has a strong heroin addiction because it mimics heroin at the synapse more closely. Li et al. (2013) show that just the cues that relate to heroin can affect brain functioning such as in the limbic system, so using a substitute drug is not going to be different from heroin in all aspects, there are other issues to consider. Methadone has been shown to help addicts to take part in other therapies such as behavioural therapy, which is a benefit of drug therapy for addiction, as explained on the Drugabuse government website. Drug dependence affects the brain chemistry and function and its effects can be long-lasting so drug therapy might help but might need other intervention as well — a main point is the drug dependence is an illness like other illnesses and needs to be treated (McLellan et al., 2000). Medication (drug therapy) can be useful as part of the treatment.

ⓔ **7 or 8/8 marks awarded.** There is accurate and thorough knowledge and understanding here given the time available for a question like this (perhaps around 12 minutes). The answer is well balanced as it looks at several concepts, theories and studies. Li et al. (2013) one of the contemporary studies in this topic area is used, as well as McLellan et al., a study that suits this key question. There is some awareness of competing arguments around the discussion of whether drug therapy is effective, which is needed for top-level marks. The answer looks at how drug therapy is useful, such as reducing side effects, and where it might not be so useful, such as needing more than drug therapy if drug addiction is a long-term illness. There is relevant evidence, such as linking to neurotransmitter functioning and showing how one opiate is likely to have similar effects at the synapse as a different opiate. There is focus on the effectiveness of drug therapy, as required by the question. There is perhaps a focus on heroin addiction rather than other types of addiction, but the answer does relate to the question, so that is acceptable here. Two drugs used in drug therapy are mentioned, which is reasonable coverage. Overall this answer is in the top level.

Practical investigation

(1) As part of your study of biological psychology you will have carried out a correlation including using the Spearman rank correlation coefficient.

(a) How did you operationalise your variables so that you could collect relevant data? (2 marks)

ⓔ There are 2 points-based AO1 marks. You need to show what you measured for the correlation and how the data were gathered.

> **Student answer**
>
> I used self-report data to find out someone's attitude to drug use and I asked them their age. I asked them to tick their age-range, to be more ethical than asking their actual age, ✓ and I asked them some Likert-type questions about their attitude to drug use. One statement was 'I think drug-taking is irresponsible' — strongly agree, agree, don't know, disagree, strongly disagree. This was the self-report data. The higher their 'drug taking is irresponsible' score the older their age would be — that was my hypothesis. ✓

ⓔ **2/2 marks awarded.** This answer clearly gives detail about the measures that were used for the correlation, though actual age ranges could be given.

(b) Explain the result of your correlation, including whether it was significant or not, and at what level of significance. (2 marks)

ⓔ There are 2 points-based AO1 marks. Give the results of the inferential testing in your correlation and explain them.

> **Student answer**
>
> My correlation did work and I rejected the null hypothesis. I used 10 participants and my Spearman's result was +0.72 which shows a positive correlation between age and condemnation of drug taking. ✓ The result was significant for a one-tailed test at $p \leq 0.01$. ✓

ⓔ **2/2 marks awarded.** This answer clearly gives detail about the result of the correlation. The examiner can check that for n=10 a result of 0.72 is significant for a one-tailed test at the level of significance given, which it is. From that point on this answer will get the 2 marks as it is clear that this student understands this part of method for the course.

Issues and debates (A-level only, Papers 1 and 3)

(1) Evaluate research methods in psychology in relation to how much we can learn about human behaviour coming from our nature or from our nurture. (12 marks)

e This question is worth 12 marks (6 AO1 and 6 AO3) and it is levels based. You need to focus on research methods rather than theory. Consider research methods that can show us about biological explanations (nature) for our behaviour and research methods that can show us about environmental (nurture) explanations for our behaviour. You will get marks for describing the research methods when you discuss them, so you do not need to spend a lot of time describing them. Discuss strengths and weaknesses of the research methods (this is evaluating them) focusing on how good (or not) they are in uncovering biological explanations for our behaviour compared with learning explanations. 'Evaluate' requires a judgement and conclusion.

Student answer

Twin studies help in understanding which characteristics come from our nature and which from our nurture, and characteristics guide our behaviour. Brendgen et al. (2005) found that physical aggression tends to be linked to genes, because they found MZ twins shared physical aggression ratings more than DZ twins and MZ twins share their genes more too. However, social aggression showed less difference so might come more from environmental influences. Twin studies help to pinpoint any genetic influences because they can offer a unique experiment in that MZ and DZ twins both share their environment and are both the same age and so on, but only MZ twins share 100% of their genes, DZ twins just share 50% of their genes. However, their environments can be different, they might have different friends, for example, and be in different classes at school, so there can be nurture influences at work. Brendgen et al. found just that — that there are both nature and nurture influences on behaviour.

Learning theorists like Skinner, Watson and Bandura, focused only on nurture because they wanted to measure observable behaviour to see how learning takes place. For example, Bandura et al. in the 1960s carried out experiments to see how far children would imitate an adult model they had seen. The researchers used a lot of controls to make sure that the imitated behaviour was measurable and isolated as an independent variable, such as having a control group and looking at gender as well as copied behaviour. They were able to form reliable conclusions because of the controls, such as making sure the children were equal in aggression before the imitative aggression was looked for. There was perhaps a lack of credibility in that the adults hit the Bobo doll in measurable ways to help the observers to record imitative aggression, but this can be said to lack ecological validity. The children may have thought they ought to imitate what they saw, and such aggression may not have occurred in real life. Experiments can have reliability but can lose out on validity, which means they may not manage to measure true human behaviour.

Learning theories look at nurture and its effects on behaviour, such as observational learning tested by Bandura, and operant conditioning developed by Skinner, also in the 1960s. Skinner's experiments tend to be reliable. They are repeated often and animals put in a situation where they can get a reward for a certain behaviour repeatedly do the behaviour to get the reward. So experiments like Bandura's with humans and Skinner's with animals are useful in finding out about nurture and its effect on human behaviour. Skinner's work with animals has been criticised as lacking generalisability to humans, though therapies that use a reward system are used with humans, such as token economy and CBT, so perhaps there is generalisability.

What learning theory experiments do not focus on is nature and any effect on learning. They just pick out observable behaviour, which does not include biological aspects of behaviour. Scanning can help to study biological aspects of behaviour, such as Raine et al.'s (1997) study of 'murderers' to see if there were brain differences compared with controls. Raine et al. did find brain differences, using PET scanning. Scanning has reliability in that there are pictures of the brain that can be measured over and over again to check for accuracy. The sample was made up of people pleading not guilty by reason of insanity and the aggression was real, so there was some validity in the sample. This study using neuroimaging is taken to give firm results that aggression at least to an extent has biological underpinnings.

It seems that experiments, PET scans and twin studies have reliability, even though there is some doubt about validity, at least to an extent. All three methods can look at the influence of nature and nurture on human behaviour. Scans seem to be more valid. It seems as if some research methods, like twin studies and scanning, are good to look at the influence of nature on behaviour and some methods, like experiments, including experiments with animals, are good for looking at the nurture side of behaviour. Brendgen et al.'s twin study shows both nature and nurture to be involved, so that seems to be the best method for looking at how far nature or nurture affects behaviour like aggression.

(e) **10–12/12 marks awarded.** The top level for this type of question requires accurate and thorough knowledge and understanding. There is a lot of knowledge and understanding here, so that is good. There is a requirement for lines of argument to be supported by evidence, and to an extent that too is the case. Each of the points of development have some evidence for the claim made. There should be the skills of integrating — and to an extent that happens as the research methods are summarised more towards the end. There is relevant evidence for each of the three methods used, and the answer does draw together ideas that show development so the answer responds to the question. There is a conclusion and a judgement at the end, and the answer focuses on research methods that aim to find out about nature or nurture, or both, with regard to human behaviour, so the mark is in the top level — Level 4.

◼ Learning theories

Overview

(1) **For each of the types of learning — classical, operant and social learning — give a real-life example of how learning would take place.** (3 marks)

ⓔ There are 3 points-based AO1 marks. This question requires you to show understanding of the three types of learning and asks for a practical application of that understanding. Only the examples are needed — no explanation of the theories — but the question asks for 'how learning would take place' so some explanation is required as well as the example.

> **Student answer**
>
> An example of classical conditioning is being afraid of lifts. Being trapped can give an automatic example of fear. Being trapped in a lift can transfer that basic fear to lifts. ✓ An example of operant conditioning is a dog barking for a biscuit. When the dog first barks, the reward of a biscuit is given and soon the dog learns to bark for the reward, which is positive reinforcement. ✓ An example of social learning is a small girl brushing her hair like her mother brushes her hair. The behaviour would come from the girl observing her mother and then performing the observed behaviour. ✓

ⓔ **3/3 marks awarded.** This answer gives an example for each type of learning and explains the example to show how it suits the type of learning in each case. The answer clearly shows knowledge and understanding, not just 'learned' knowledge, and that is what AO1 tests, so this is a good answer.

Content

(1) **What is meant by extinction and spontaneous recovery with regard to classical conditioning?** (2 marks)

ⓔ There are 2 points-based AO1 marks. There is 1 mark for each definition.

> **Student answer**
>
> Extinction occurs when a previously learned association no longer produces the response to the stimulus. This happens after the pairing no longer occurs for a while — the stimulus then does not produce the response. ✓ However, sometimes for no apparent reason the stimulus, after extinction, starts producing the response again, which is called spontaneous recovery. The response appears spontaneously, which means not planned, and so is recovered. ✓

ⓔ **2/2 marks awarded.** There is enough in each case for the 1 mark and the understanding of the two terms is clear. An example can help to elaborate to be sure of a mark so is often worth including.

(2) Assess one therapy for phobias, based on learning theories.   (8 marks)

e There are 8 levels-based marks: 4 AO1 and 4 AO3. This is an essay question (called 'extended open response'). 'Assess' involves giving consideration to factors that relate to the question and then showing which are important. You need to make a judgement.

> **Student answer**
>
> Systematic desensitisation is more ethical than other treatments for phobias because it is a gradual treatment and the person helps to set the procedure involved. Flooding is another treatment drawing on learning theory, which involves immersing someone in their fear. This is less ethical, causing more distress. BPS guidelines include responsibility, which is about the principle of no harm.
>
> Systematic desensitisation, as well as being ethical, has been shown to be successful by studies such as Capafóns et al. (1998), who used it and found it helped people with their phobia of flying. Inglesias and Inglesias (2013) found systematic desensitisation had worked in a real case, where someone had a phobia for driving on a specific interstate road in the USA.
>
> However, the treatment is only successful for those who are able to relax successfully and maintain that relaxation, which might not apply to everyone. Also it is not a treatment that rests only on classical conditioning as claimed, because it involves cognitive elements such as positive thinking while relaxing. Toozandehjani (2011) used interviews and self-report data to find out about the effectiveness of therapy. It was found that systematic desensitisation with assertive training was more effective than the two separately, suggesting systematic desensitisation is effective, but it helps to have another focus as well.
>
> In conclusion, as systematic desensitisation is reasonably ethical, the individual has some control, and there are studies that show its effectiveness, it is considered a useful therapy for phobias. It draws on principles of classical conditioning, where a learned fear response is replaced with a relaxation response, so it is a therapy based on learning theory. However, there are cognitive elements too and it has been found to be effective when combined with other treatment as well such as assertiveness training. It is judged to be effective and useful, with some reservations, such as not being suitable for everyone.

e **8/8 marks awarded.** Page 43 of the A-level specimen answer materials (available on the Edexcel website) gives the levels mark scheme for an 'assess' 8-mark question. The highest level asks for accurate and thorough knowledge and understanding, which is found in this answer. There is not much pure description, but the answer shows clear knowledge and understanding about this treatment. The highest level also asks for a well-developed and logical assessment, which is also found here. The conclusion helps. The rest of the answer is evaluation, which is good, but it is the final paragraph that adds the element of 'assessing', which is necessary. The answer has to 'demonstrate awareness of significant competing arguments' and must lead to a 'balanced judgement being presented'. That is the case in this answer. There could be other material, however, in the time available (in general allow 1 minute for each mark, but for extended open-response questions like this, you can add a few minutes, so about 12 minutes for this answer) this is a top-level answer.

Method (also A-level Paper 3)

(1) Evaluate observation as a research method in psychology. (12 marks)

ⓔ This question is worth 12 marks (6 AO1 and 6 AO3) and it is levels based. This is an essay question. 'Evaluate' requires you to 'review information then bring it together to form a conclusion, drawing on evidence including strengths, weaknesses, alternative actions, relevant data or information. Come to a supported judgement of a subject's qualities and relation to its context' (this is from page 78 of the A-level specification). Use as much evaluation as you can, and the AO1 element, the knowledge and understanding, will be seen as you evaluate. You do not need to spend time describing the method.

Student answer

Observations can be overt, those being observed are aware of the study, or they can be covert, they are not aware that they are being studied. Participant observation means that the observer is part of the situation. Non-participant observation means that the observer is set apart from the situation. Naturalistic observations take place in the participant's environment, while structured observations are set up. Observations can gather qualitative data when open questions are asked such as making notes about someone's opinions. And they can gather quantitative data, such as tallying certain behaviours like children playing with a certain toy. Often both types of data are collected. A strength of observations is when more than one observer watches the same behaviour, using the same categories, because if their observations match there is inter-observer reliability. Also if it is a participant observation there can be good validity, as the observer can access all the data and it is 'real life' — which is the good point about naturalistic observations. One problem can be that generalisability is difficult because a naturalistic observation tends to be about one group of participants, and a different group can yield different data because there are fewer controls than there are in an experiment. Structured observations have the strength of having a set up a procedure which is replicable and so reliability is likely, whereas naturalistic observations, though more valid and based on real life, are less replicable because of being natural. Structured observations, for example, can have careful situational controls. Psychology benefits from observational data because although there can be some controls, unlike experiments, observations tend to be more valid in that someone's real behaviour is being watched even if the situation is set up. One advantage of structured observations is that they can help when a situation does not happen often so it is not realistic to wait for it to happen so that it can be observed. This could be something like a cyclist riding on the pavement and waiting to see what pedestrians would do. It might be more efficient to set the situation up and then watch. As observations can gather both qualitative and quantitative data, they can involve triangulation, where data from different sources can be compared, which can help with both validity and reliability.

> Observations can involve some interpretation about what to record and when, but if time and event sampling are used, there would be more objectivity. Given that observations can be tested for reliability, they gather empirical data, they can have objectivity, and any quantitative data can be carefully analysed (e.g. using a Chi-squared test), they are a scientific method, which psychology aims for. However, there is an element of qualitative data and interpretation perhaps, which means a less scientific approach, nonetheless more validity perhaps and a more holistic approach than other methods.

ⓔ **10/12 marks awarded.** This answer demonstrates accurate and thorough knowledge and understanding of observations as a research method, which puts it into Level 4, the top level. However, although there are a lot of evaluation points, they are not well-organised and so the answer is not very well-developed or logical. There is some planning as pure description comes at the start — though not necessary, this can be one way of planning an essay. Evaluation points follow. There is some logic in dealing with the usual evaluation issues — validity, reliability, objectivity, type of data and so on. There is an awareness of competing arguments when the balance of qualitative and quantitative data is explored and there is comparison with experiments. There is a balanced conclusion in that the method is said to be mainly scientific but with an element of holism involved. Overall, Level 4 is reached, but the slight lack of chains of reasoning and logical order of points means it would probably only receive 10 marks. Of course in an actual examination, this might get 12 marks. Page 57 of the A-level specimen answer materials (available on the Edexcel website) gives you the levels used for a 12-mark question like this.

(2) An observation of helping behaviour in a shopping mall showed that more males than females held doors open for other shoppers. Tallying was carried out, recording not only the gender of those helping (holding the door open for someone else) but also the gender of those being helped (those going through the door). It was necessary only to record helping behaviour when one person held the door and one person came through, so if more than one person came through that incident was not recorded. No other information was recorded. A test was done on the results, which were found not to be significant at $p \leq 0.05$.

Gender of person being helped	Gender of helper		
	Male	Female	Total
Male	12	4	16
Female	18	8	26
Total	30	12	42

Table of results for the study, showing number of those helping and those helped with regard to gender

(a) What test would be needed for this study? Give three reasons why this test would be chosen. (2 marks)

(This part (a) question is not for AS.)

(e) There are 2 points-based AO2 marks. You could get 1 mark for naming the test and one reason and 1 mark for the other two reasons.

Student answer

The test is the Chi-squared. This is the test for looking for a difference ✓ when the data are nominal and it is an independent groups design. ✓

(e) **2/2 marks awarded.** The test is correct with three correct reasons so maximum marks here.

(b) Explain one example of where a control would have been useful. (2 marks)

(e) There are 2 points-based marks, 1 AO2 and 1 AO3. The AO2 mark is for applying your knowledge and understanding to the study, the AO3 mark is for developing and refining practical procedures and designs. There are problems built into the study so choose one and show where a control would have worked to improve the study. For 2 marks say enough to show good understanding of the issue. When you are asked to 'explain' give the point and then justify your answer.

Student answer

It would have been useful to know whether the shopper was weighed down with bags or not, and whether they had a hand free to open the door for themselves ✓ as this could have made people more likely to hold the door open for them regardless of gender. This was a possible extraneous variable that needed to be noted or controlled. ✓

(e) **2/2 marks awarded.** There is 1 mark for refining the study by suggesting recording what the shopper was carrying and 1 mark for relating the idea to how it would affect the findings of the study. Note the use of the term 'extraneous variable' which shows good knowledge and understanding.

(c) Explain one ethical issue with this study. (2 marks)

(e) There are 2 points-based AO2 marks. Naturalistic observations like this one are special with regard to ethics, so this is an interesting question. As with all 'explain' questions, you need to describe the issue and then justify it (link to this study).

Student answer

One problem with observations is that there can be no informed consent, so the study is always going to be unethical. BPS guidelines ask for informed consent for every study.

(e) **0/2 marks awarded.** This answer gains 0 marks because observations are permitted if the behaviour occurs in a public place where someone might expect to be observed, as is the case here. It would be difficult to carry out observations otherwise. If someone is in a public place and all other ethical issues are observed, then observing them without recording personal information (which would not be known) is seen as ethical.

(d) The test was found not to be significant at $p \leq 0.05$. Explain what this means. (2 marks)

ℯ There are 2 points-based AO2 marks. The question is about levels of significance. Explain what the phrase $p \leq 0.05$ means and what it means to say that the study is not significant at that level. 'Explain' requires you to give the point and then justify/link it to the study.

| Student answer |

$p \leq 0.05$ means that the probability that the results are due to chance is equal to or less than 5%. ✓ Saying that the results are not significant at that level means there is a greater than 5% probability of the results being due to chance so the null hypothesis would not be rejected. ✓ $p \leq 0.05$ is the most generous level of significance where results are accepted in psychology.

ℯ **2/2 marks awarded.** This gains the marks as the answer shows clear understanding of the 5% level of significance and what it means to say that level is not achieved.

Studies

(1) Describe the aims of Watson and Rayner (1920) and one study from Becker et al. (2002), Bastian et al. (2011) or Capafóns et al. (1998). (4 marks)

ℯ There are 4 points-based AO1 marks. The question focuses on the classic study in learning theories and one of the three contemporary studies. Be ready to pick out the study you have learned about, and not to be put off by seeing named studies you may not know about. The aims are what the researchers set out to achieve. As there are 2 marks for each study's aims, you need to write quite a bit in each case.

| Student answer |

Watson and Rayner (1920) carried out what is known as the Little Albert study. The aim was to see if the principles of classical conditioning could be used to give a phobia in a human baby. ✓ They wanted to condition the baby to fear what he had previously enjoyed playing with. Becker et al. (2002) carried out a study in Fiji. They wanted to look at the role of the media, specifically television, on eating behaviour, to test the claim that observational learning can take place. ✓ They aimed to use Fiji girls as participants, just as television was being introduced, and to ask them about their attitudes to eating and food and then to ask them 3 years later to see if their attitudes had changed — as well as finding out their television watching habits. They wanted to see if watching television and having television role models would affect their attitudes to diet and eating. ✓

ℯ **3/4 marks awarded.** This answer has a lot of information. However, the second sentence about the Watson and Rayner (1920) study is not quite detailed or different enough from the first to get a second mark. A second sentence could be added, such as: 'They wanted to condition the baby to fear what he had previously enjoyed playing with. Specifically they wanted to see if causing fear by striking a metal bar behind the baby's head would lead to association between the fear from the noise and the pet rat the baby had previously been playing with happily.' The detail of the second study's aims is better.

Key question

(1) Explain a key question for society using two concepts from learning theories.   (6 marks)

ⓔ There are 6 points-based AO1 marks. These are AO1 marks, knowledge and understanding, as the question is asking about a key question you will have prepared. You may not have prepared using two concepts specifically, but just choose two of the ones you have looked at.

Student answer

One key question is whether role models have an influence on whether someone develops anorexia nervosa or not. One concept from the learning approach is identification. When someone identifies with a role model they are likely to imitate their behaviour. ✓ Studies by Bandura (1961, 1963, 1965) have shown that girls copy female models and boys copy male models, so if female role models are slim then girls are likely to want to be slim. ✓ If someone observes behaviour but does not identify with the role model they are not so likely to perform the behaviour. ✓ Girls who want to be slim are likely to stop eating and can develop eating disorders such as anorexia. Another concept from the learning approach is reinforcement. If a role model is reinforced for being slim, such as praised, paid more or featured a lot in the media, then they might be imitated more. ✓ Studies by Bandura suggest that behaviour that is rewarded is likely to be imitated more, such as in vicarious learning (and that seeing someone punished can stop behaviour). ✓ There is also negative reinforcement for being fat, through criticism and teasing. So not wanting to be fat to avoid criticism, and wanting to be slim to get praise, might be two types of reinforcement that help to explain anorexia. ✓

ⓔ **6/6 marks awarded.** This is thorough and answers the question clearly, giving two named concepts and sticking with them. It is as much the structuring of this answer that gets the full marks as the amount of information. One concept is 'identification' which is the idea of copying role models that someone associates with. The other concept is 'reinforcement' which is broad enough to cover a lot of different issues. Choosing this broader category has helped the answer by enabling it to have depth.

Practical investigation

(1) You will have carried out an observation within the learning approach. Answer the following questions using your study.

(a) How did you gather the quantitative data when doing your observation?   (2 marks)

ⓔ There are 2 points-based AO1 marks. AO1 is chosen here as you are recalling what you did rather than applying or evaluating. You need to explain to the reader what you did, and be sure to talk about gathering quantitative not qualitative data.

Student answer

I made tally marks according to the gender of any child playing in the book corner and the gender of any child playing on the climbing frame. There was one mark for each act of playing in those ways, and the mark went in the relevant gender box, boy or girl. ✓✓

ⓔ 2/2 marks awarded. This answer is detailed and clear. The reader can tell that the observation is about gender and play, and the focus is on playing in the book corner as opposed to playing on the climbing frame. It would be assumed that this is in a nursery or somewhere like that. Tallying is clearly gathering quantitative data, which answers the question. Then the answer shows 'how' the data were gathered, which is what is required. One tally for anyone playing in either of those places/ways, and different boxes for gender as well.

(b) To what extent was your study credible? (4 marks)

ⓔ There are 4 points-based AO3 marks. Expect questions you might not have prepared and be ready to use your practical investigation to answer any such question. Here you do not need to say what credibility is, but use your study to discuss its credibility. Credibility is about how far someone would accept your study and objective (scientific) credibility is how scientific the research method and procedure was, for example. Be sure to use your own study in this answer, not studies or research in general.

Student answer

My study is credible because the research method was scientific, in that quantitative data were gathered. Quantitative data can be measured in such a way that the study can be repeated so the findings can be tested for reliability. ✓ This is particularly the case if there is more than one observer and they agree, though in my study there was only me so this might mean the study is not so credible. ✓ Also quantitative data can be analysed using statistical testing, which is a scientific way of finding out to what extent the results are due to chance. I used a Chi-squared test on my results and found they were significant at $p \leq 0.05$, which means I rejected my null hypothesis. ✓ Another feature of science that my study used was reductionism — I looked at gender and play by focusing on just two pieces of apparatus so that I could make clear observations that did not rely on interpretation. ✓

ⓔ 4/4 marks awarded. This answer brings in a lot of the element of science. There is mention of reliability, inter-rater reliability (lack of), statistical testing (elaborated to give detail, which may well have got another mark) and reductionism. Using terms appropriately is helpful for getting marks. The answer is well focused on the practical investigation throughout and well focused on the question — credibility is the only focus. Note as well that quite a lot of information is given for each mark.

(c) Explain one problem with your study and how you might have addressed it? (4 marks)

e There are 4 points-based AO3 marks. Expect questions in the examination that ask you to refine procedures either in an unseen study given as stimulus material in the exam or relating to your own or another study you have covered. This question asks you not only to talk about one problem you came across but also to suggest what would have helped to solve the problem. Check questions and if they have more than one focus, be sure to address the whole question. It can be useful to re-read the question after you have answered it, so that you can add more detail if you realise that your answer does not cover all that is required.

Student answer

One problem with my study was working out which child was a boy and which was a girl when doing my observation. I observed children aged between 3 and 4 and they were often dressed in trousers. ✓ It was not clear from haircuts either which were boys and which were girls. I should have asked a member of staff where I was not sure as that would make my study more accurate. ✓ I noted down something about the child such as colour of jumper and aimed to ask staff later but I did not get the chance to do this. ✓ I think I got the gender right, but not being sure about it possibly meant my tallying was not always accurate, which would have affected the study. ✓

---

e **4/4 marks awarded.** The problem is clear and is an understandable one. The question does not ask for a problem that should have been thought about, but it is clear that this student had thought about it and had intended to do something about it. The elaboration on the issue is what earns the additional marks. The suggested solution, which had been attempted, is a sensible one and the whole answer shows understanding of the study, the importance of controls, the problem and a possible solution.

Issues and debates (A-level only, Papers 1 and 3)

(1) Psychology has changed over time, from its beginnings with Wundt's laboratory studies looking at memory in 1879 to current focuses. Not only has the subject matter of psychology changed, but so have the methods used to study that subject matter. One change, for example, is that most early psychologists were men and now many are women, including presidents of the most important psychological organisations.

Evaluate, using concepts, theories and studies in biological psychology and learning theories, how psychology has developed over time. You must make reference to the context in your answer.

(12 marks)

e This question is worth 12 marks and it is levels based. You need to give knowledge and understanding (AO1 4 marks), application to the stimulus material (AO2 4 marks), and evaluation about the issues (AO3 4 marks) in about equal measures. When you have a source like this, you will know that AO2 is involved, and if AO2 is involved then a 12-mark question will be split three ways with regard to the assessment objectives as is done here. You need to bring in both topic areas and should aim to bring in studies, theories and concepts as far as possible. The stimulus material points you to changes in psychology itself and in the methods used, so that would be two good areas to focus on in your answer. 'Evaluate' needs a judgement and conclusion.

Student answer

Biological psychology uses scanning. fMRI can see the brain in action which MRI scanning, used previously could not. fMRI is non-invasive and is safe, quite easy for someone to use and can uncover good detail of the brain. MRI could not measure the functioning of the brain and neuroimaging has moved on from its early beginnings, showing the development of psychology over time.

William James wanted to understand why animals and humans had developed into what they were in his day (1842–1910). This school of thinking is called functionalism — which no longer exists but now there is evolutionary psychology, which draws on Darwin's ideas. This shows that there is development over time, but not to the extent that older ideas are completely rejected.

Freud emphasised the unconscious part of the mind and psychoanalysis is still used as a therapy today, showing that there has been development (such as the focus on object relations, which emphasises early attachment and upbringing, building on Freud's ideas) but that the basics remain.

Behaviourism, which covers learning theories, including the work of Watson and Skinner, was focused on from the early 1900s to the present day, with a lot of the work taking place in the 1960s. Watson and Rayner in 1920 used classical conditioning principles to condition a fear in a young baby and treatment like systematic desensitisation, which uses the same principles in reverse (replacing the fear response with a relaxation response) is still in use today. Systematic desensitisation has been shown to be successful by studies such as Capafóns et al. (1998), who used it to cure people of their phobia of flying and Inglesias and Inglesias (2013) who found systematic desensitisation worked in a real case, where someone had a phobia for driving on a specific interstate road in the USA. This shows that perhaps psychology has not changed over time as much as might be thought — classical conditioning principles, first developed by Pavlov (1927) are still important today.

@ **8/12 marks awarded.** The top level for this type of question asks for accurate and thorough knowledge and understanding. There is a lot of knowledge and understanding here, so that is good. There is also a requirement for lines of argument to be supported by evidence, and to an extent that too is the case in this answer. Each of the points of development has some evidence for the claim made and the answer does draw together ideas that show development so responds to the question. However, there should also be the skill of integrating — this seems to be missing as this answer is a list, albeit a good one. Therefore the answer does not fall into the top level. There is no conclusion or judgement at the end, though there are some within the answer. Level 3 seems appropriate for this answer.

Knowledge check answers

1 Example: receptors are found at the end of the dendrites of a neuron and are there to receive, as the name suggests, a neurotransmitter (chemical) from other neurons. A receptor has a specific shape that the neurotransmitter chemical will either fit or not fit into. If there is a fit, the message is passed on from the receptor as a chemical, to the cell body. So neurotransmitters are chemicals that are used to send messages around the brain (the brain, along with the spinal cord, makes up the central nervous system) and they fit some receptors but not others. Neurotransmitters sit at terminal buttons at the end of the axon of a neuron, and they are released from there, received by another neuron at the dendrites, travelling to the cell body and then the message proceeds by means of an electrical impulse from that cell body, travelling down the axon. The synapse is the gap between the terminal button of one neuron and the dendrite of another.

2 Scanning uses active human brains, so there is validity and an element of real life about the method. Animals are not humans — there are differences, so findings from animal studies might not be valid. Animals that are studied are often brain damaged to look at particular brain processing, so the animals are not doing their usual functioning, which lacks validity. Scanning produces images that can be measured and checked by more than one person so there can be reliability, though animal studies can yield data that can be checked, so they do not lack reliability in that sense. Animal brains are scanned to get evidence, so the two methods are mixed, not always separate. Both methods have information that is valuable, notwithstanding any ethical arguments.

3 Nicotine works in a way that means more dopamine is in the reward pathway in the brain and dopamine gives pleasure. Nicotine can trigger a message in a neuron as it mimics (acts like) acetylcholine, binding to the same receptors and triggering dopamine. Cocaine works differently. Cocaine blocks the reuptake of dopamine, also in the reward pathway, and so there is more dopamine in the synapse, remaining there to give more pleasure.

4 Raine et al. (1997) showed that those who pleaded guilty to murder by reason of insanity, which was about emotional impulsive violence, had prefrontal cortex differences when compared with controls. Bechara and van der Linden in 2005 found that prefrontal lobes regulate behaviour and mean there is planning and deferred rewards. If the prefrontal lobe area is damaged this does seem to lead to more negative emotions, which can be about being aggressive. Raine et al.'s study was well controlled and used careful scanning which could give objective measures.

5 Three pieces of evidence are:

- A stimulated hypothalamus and basal ganglia (part of the limbic system) in cats gives the animals aggressive seizures (Andy and Velamati, 1978).
- Downer (1961) found that a removed amygdala meant abnormal functioning in response to visual stimuli, with a more calm behaviour than their usual reactions.
- Swantje et al. (2012) found that the smaller the amygdala (measured using MRI scanning) the more self-reported aggression there was.

6 Darwin noticed that some organisms (such as birds) had features/characteristics that were useful in their environment. There were differences in species that suited an organism, such as for finding food. He thought that genes survived through reproduction and only those organisms that were suited to their environment would survive to reproduce. This was survival of the fittest — the fittest (most suitable) characteristics and features would be passed on through reproduction. In humans an example is aggression. For example, males show aggression to other males to protect 'their' female (Buss and Shackleton, 1997).

7 Barzman et al. (2013) found that cortisol in boys' saliva in the morning correlated with more aggressive acts as recorded by nurses, suggesting that cortisol and aggression go together. They also found that the levels of DHEA and testosterone after waking up correlated with the amount of aggression in the first recorded aggressive incident of the day. Dabbs et al. (1987) showed that levels of testosterone of male prisoners predicted their level of aggression. Those with high testosterone levels were rated as 'tough' by peers. High levels of testosterone in the saliva linked to the prisoner being involved in violent crime and vice versa (low testosterone levels linked with non-violent crime).

8 Credibility has a number of linked meanings mainly focused around scientific method. Reliable, objective data, for example, are credible (believable) data, and trustworthy researchers using scientific methods are credible researchers. If research involves subjectivity it is less credible and if it is valid it is credible. Two criticisms of Freud's work are:

- Freud's findings tended to lack empirical data and he did not use overtly scientific methods, so his work is said to lack credibility. In many ways his studies are not replicable, and science needs to replicate findings.
- Freud interpreted the data from his clients so could be said to use subjectivity, and as objectivity is required for findings to be credible, Freud's findings can be seen as lacking credibility.

9 +0.62 is likely to be a significant correlation and to show a strong relationship because it is closer to +1 (which is a perfect relationship). The '+' sign shows that this is a positive relationship — as one variable rises, the other variable rises as well. −0.57

is also quite a strong correlation, though not quite as strong as 0.62. It is likely to be significant but you can say that in a lot of cases the relationship was not really found. The '–' sign shows this is a negative correlation — as one score rises, the other falls.

10 Example: a positive correlation is when two scores vary together and as one score rises (e.g. temperature) the other one rises too (e.g. aggression measured by horn hooting in a city). A negative correlation is when two scores vary together and as one score rises (e.g. temperature) the other one falls (e.g. how often someone goes outside).

11 CAT scanning uses x-rays and they are dangerous for humans, including linking to cancers, so such scanning should not be used often and as a method of studying the brain it would not be recommended. PET scanning uses fairly broad imaging and cannot pinpoint exact brain areas so though it is useful, for such complex functioning, there are limitations. fMRI scanning cannot look at the actual receptors of neurotransmitters so there are limitations (but it has a lot of strengths too, such as being very precise).

12 Twin studies compare MZ with DZ twins to look for differences in characteristics that might then be attributed to genetic differences. Adoption studies are different as they focus on children who have been adopted and compare the adoptive environment and its effects with the biological effects by looking at biological parents too. So they focus on environment versus biology whereas twin studies tend to focus more on biology. Another difference is that adoption studies tend to occur over time, because it takes time for a characteristic to develop in a child and then there can be a looking back to the biological parents' characteristics. Twin studies can be longitudinal and often are, but they can also study current characteristics and events.

13 Raine et al. (1997) found brain differences in people who pleaded not guilty to murder by reason of insanity. They found differences, for example, in the prefrontal cortex compared to a control group who had not been charged with murder. The study was carefully done, using matched controls and scanning which can give objective measurements that are reliable. If someone has differences in the brain we might say they are not responsible for their behaviour in the same way that they would be held responsible if a crime was premeditated. Betts in 2009 suggested that a case where a man strangled his wife (aggressive behaviour) could have been due to brain damage and CAT scanning was used to gather the evidence. Matthies et al. (2012) used MRI scanning and showed that the size of the amygdala related to the life-time aggression score, showing links between brain structure and aggression. These studies suggest that human behaviour can come from brain differences which might then be said to be not something they can control or 'help'.

14 Social learning theory. Social learning theory and operant conditioning. Classical conditioning.

15 Negative reinforcement means that a behaviour is repeated, just as positive reinforcement does. They are the same thing except that in positive reinforcement the behaviour is repeated because of something good being given, whereas in negative reinforcement the behaviour is repeated because something bad is taken away. For example, if someone goes to a second friend's house to avoid noise in the first friend's house, their behaviour (which house to go to) is reinforced by avoiding the unwanted loud noise. Negative punishment means that a behaviour stops, so this is the opposite of negative reinforcement (which means that a behaviour occurs). Negative punishment can mean something good is taken away. (Positive punishment is when something bad is given.)

16 AMEA stands for **A**lternative theory, **M**ethod, **E**vidence, **A**pplication. With regard to the evaluation of social learning theory, there is: the alternative theory that biological factors such as hormones or brain structure might affect behaviour rather than it coming from observational learning; methodological evaluation such as that laboratory experiments are often used and an artificial and controlled setting may not yield valid data; evidence from Bandura's work in the laboratory, showing that children tend to copy aggressive models, especially those with certain features, such as the same gender; application in that the 9 o'clock watershed has been put into place to try to limit children's viewing of violence on television.

17 1961: the independent variables were whether there was aggression or no aggression, also bringing in the gender of the model. 1963: the independent variables were whether the aggression was modelled by a real-life model, a film of the real-life model, or a cartoon model. 1965: the independent variables were whether the model was punished, rewarded or there were no consequences, with an additional variable of directly rewarding the children for reproducing the behaviour.

18 The first steps are that the person is taught deep muscle relaxation and they work out a hierarchy of their fears with the therapist — this gives a step-by-step way of working from the least feared aspect of planes to the most feared (perhaps a picture of a plane, to going to the airport, to sitting in a simulator, to sitting on a plane, to taxiing and so on). Then each step is introduced, with the relaxation, so that the pairing of the step and the relaxation can take place, replacing the fear response. Gradually this goes on right up to the most feared situation (taking off perhaps).

19 Systematic desensitisation (SD) is a good therapy for certain issues such as phobias. Issues that might have come about through classical conditioning seem to be best dealt with using classical

conditioning principles, which SD uses. It is based clearly on principles that are evidenced from studies such as Pavlov's so there is a clear rationale behind the therapy, which makes it a good one. The client has some power too, as they work out the hierarchy that will suit them and they also have the power to choose what to be exposed to, which is a more ethical therapy than flooding, which drops them into the deep end.

20 Both use classical conditioning principles, which is a similarity. Systematic desensitisation is more ethical than flooding because it is less stressful, taking place over time, for example. Also it is more ethical because the individual has control over the hierarchy and their relaxation whereas in flooding the person is left to face their fear. Willis and Edwards (1969) showed that systematic desensitisation is more successful than flooding (implosion therapy) in reducing the fear of mice and they found the effects of the systematic desensitisation was still present after 7 weeks. However, in 1971 Boulourgouris et al. found that flooding was better than systematic desensitisation and the effects lasted over 12 months. Therefore, there is evidence both ways, so they are comparable in that it is hard to show one is more effective than the other.

21 A non-participant overt observation.

22 A non-participant observation. Or you could say a covert observation, because then the observer does not have to deal with participant expectations.

23 Inter-researcher reliability can be found, which means more than one person carrying out a content analysis of the material that is being studied and them all finding the same results. This means there is reliability, which is a strength of a study.

24 Animals can be used daily and procedures carried out daily over a period of time, which would not be practicable with humans. Also if generations are to be studied, animals like mice are useful as their gestation period is relatively short, whereas this is not practicable when using humans. Animals, however, do not have the same brain structure or cognitive processing as humans, so generalising from findings from animal laboratory studies to humans is not really possible. Also human lives are complex, so isolating variables in a laboratory — as you can with animals — might not have relevance to the complexity of human behaviour.

25 Animals can be used to develop drugs that can help humans, so ethically their use is justified if the ends justify the means. Also the animal species can be helped using the knowledge obtained from experiments they are part of. Although there are strong principles for using animals in laboratory research and they must be adhered to, there are still procedures that can be done that cannot be done to humans for ethical reasons, so ethically, to protect our own species, we can say that work with animals is justified.

26 A test of difference (not a correlation), nominal data (not ordinal, interval or ratio) and using an independent groups design (not repeated measures or matched pairs).

27 $p \leq 0.01$ means that the probability of the results being due to chance (p) is equal to or less than ($\leq$) 1% or 1 in 100 (0.01). So 1 in 100 of the results might be due to chance but 99 out of 100 results (or that proportion) will not be due to chance.

28 Nominal data: whether female or male, and whether they can do the test or not.

29 There will be no significant difference in gender with regard to who goes up to the large-screen televisions (over 36 inch), and it is not the case that more men will do so than women. The IV is gender (whether the person is male or female). The DV is going up to the large-screen televisions.

30 For example: one theme might be 'being alone' as that suits the idea of the child 'standing alone' and also them 'not mixing with other children'. 'Turning away' might suit 'being alone'. 'Walking to another area' sounds more active though, rather than passively 'standing alone'. A theme there might be 'avoiding other children' and 'not watching other children playing' could be 'avoiding other children' as well. This picks out two themes ('being alone' and 'avoiding other children').

31 There were issues with ethics in that the stimulus used (the noise) caused a startled response in the baby, which was about distressing the baby. There was a difficulty with validity in that, although the baby was allowed to play as he might normally play, parts of the situation were artificial (e.g. having the researchers there).

32 41.3% said they had television in 1995 compared with 70.8% in 1998. 12.7% had an EAT-26 score of more than 20 in 1995 compared with 29.2% in 1998. 0% said they used self-induced vomiting to control their weight in 1995 compared with 11.3% in 1998.

33 Anorexia is about being underweight. Celebrities are seen as underweight (size 0) and are role models for young girls. Celebrities and models are praised for being thin and rewarded by such praise. Young girls identify with celebrities and want to be like them, so are motivated to imitate their behaviour. Vicarious learning is seeing someone rewarded (in this case for being thin) and so imitating the behaviour.

34 The answers depend on your own study. If you do not have notes that give you answers to this knowledge check, find out from someone else in your group or from your teacher what the answers are.

■ Glossary

This section contains definitions of the key terms that you need to know for the topics in this book: biological psychology and learning theories. They are subdivided into each approach.

The biological approach

Ablation a research method used to study the brain, to find out which part carries out which function. Ablation means a part is removed (if a part is just damaged, that is lesioning).

Action potential, see electrical impulse.

Adoption studies children who are adopted are studied, because their environment will differ from their biological family and yet they will share their genes with their biological family. So it can be seen if a characteristic is attributable to nature or nurture.

Axon this goes from the cell body of a neuron to the terminal buttons and takes the electrical impulse from one to the other. The axon has a myelin sheath as protection, and nodes of Ranvier help the impulse to pass along it speedily.

Case study a research method gathering in-depth and detailed data about one individual or a small group. Triangulation is used to find themes from all the different data sources.

Catharsis refers to Freud's idea that energy taken up to keep aggression unconscious can be released.

Cell body where the chemical message from a neurotransmitter is translated into an electrical impulse to continue the 'message'. The cell body contains the nucleus and the axon comes from it.

Central nervous system the brain and spinal cord. The brain is within the skull and the spinal cord is set within the vertebrae.

Concordance rate the extent to which pairs of twins share a characteristic.

Conscious mind the part of the mind that contains the thoughts, feelings, ideas and other aspects of thinking that the individual knows about and can access easily.

Control group in an experiment there is likely to be an experimental group that has the manipulation and a control group that does not. The control group gives a baseline measure.

Corpus callosum joins the two hemispheres of the brain, passing messages between them.

Correlation design a design in which one person generates two scores, both on a sliding scale. More than one participant is tested in this way and the two sets of scores are then tested to see if there is a relationship between them, such as one score rising as the other falls (this would be a negative correlation).

Co-variables in a correlation where two variables are tested to see if when one changes the other changes too, in relation to one another, these are co-variables — they co-vary

Credibility the extent to which the findings of research are believable. This is an important issue when doing scientific research.

Defence mechanisms strategies that help the ego to balance out the demands of the id and the superego. Some defence mechanisms push thoughts back into the unconscious and some turn them into something else to make them acceptable. Some defence mechanisms are repression, denial, projection, displacement and regression.

Dendrite from the cell body of a neuron there are dendrites at the end of which are receptors to receive neurotransmitters, sending a message to the cell body via the dendrites.

Denial a defence mechanism that explains how traumatic events seem to be ignored by the person experiencing them. By keeping the memories unconscious they do not have to face them.

Dependent variable the variable that is measured as a result of manipulation of the independent variable.

Dizygotic (DZ) twins non-identical twins from two eggs, who share 50% of their genes like any brother or sister.

Ego the second part of the personality, which works on the reality principle. It is the rational part that works to satisfy the demands of the id and the superego.

Ego ideal part of the superego. It is what each person thinks they should be like.

Electrical impulse, called an 'action potential', travels from the cell body via the axon of a neuron to release neurotransmitter into the synaptic gap.

Epigenetic modification how different environmental influences on an individual over time affect which genes are switched on and off.

Eros the life instinct, which is self-preservation and a sexual instinct; it is about biological arousal.

Evolution how inherited characteristics pass from generation to generation.

Genes the sections of DNA that make people who they are. A gene consists of a long strand of DNA, and genes are set up in such a way that they are a blueprint for what people are like.

Genotype the instruction from our genes to make us what we are.

Holistic approach the idea that to find out about something, the whole must be studied, not the parts. For example, you can study a person's levels of aggression by scanning and seeing activity in the limbic system, but real-life aggression is more complex: it has a trigger, a type (physical or verbal, for example) and a background. The opposite is holistic reductionist.

Hormones chemical messengers that work more slowly than neurotransmitters and are carried in the blood stream. They are produced by the endocrine glands including the pineal gland, pituitary gland and thyroid.

Hypothesis a statement of what is thought will happen, which is the alternate hypothesis and becomes the experimental hypothesis in an experiment. The null hypothesis states the opposite.

Id the first part of the personality, in the unconscious. It is the 'I want' part, which acts on the pleasure principle.

Independent variable the variable that is manipulated by the researcher such as giving one group a list of words with the same meaning and another group words with meanings that are not the same.

Lesioning a research method used to study the brain and what part is for what purpose. It involves damaging parts of the brain, as opposed to ablation, which means a part is actually removed. Research using lesioning is mostly done on animals or as part of a medical procedure on humans, not just for research purposes.

Lobe there are four lobes in the brain — the prefrontal, temporal, occipital and parietal lobes.

Mode of action drugs work in the brain in particular ways, mainly the focus is on how they work at the synapse.

Monozygotic (MZ) twins identical twins from one egg, who share 100% of their genes.

Myelination a covering (myelin sheath) around the nerve fibre for protection.

Nature–nurture debate the question of how far a characteristic comes from our nature (what we are born with, which is down to our genes) and how far it comes from our nurture (what we experience from our environment as we develop, which is down to our upbringing).

Negative correlation a relationship found when two scores from each participant are produced, and enough participants are tested; it shows that as one score rises the other falls. For example, as age rises speed of driving falls: a 60-year-old will drive more slowly than a 30-year-old.

Neuron where neurotransmitters/chemicals trigger electrical impulses down an axon to release more neurotransmitters.

Neurotransmitters chemicals in the brain that act as messengers and either cross from one neuron to the receptors of another neuron over the synaptic gap or do not fit the receptors so are blocked.

Nodes of Ranvier gaps in the myelin sheath, which insulates the axon of a neuron.

Positive correlation a relationship found when two scores from each participant are produced, and enough participants are tested; it shows that as one score rises

the other rises too. For example, as age rises, the time taken to react to a stimulus rises. A 60-year-old will take longer to react than a 30-year-old, for example.

Post-synaptic neuron the neuron having the dendrites with receptors receiving the message.

Preconscious mind the part of the mind that contains thoughts and ideas that the individual can access although they are not currently conscious.

Pre-synaptic neuron the neuron sending its message down the axon to the terminal buttons.

Randomising when an experiment requires two groups randomisation of participants into the two groups can help with fairness.

Receptors places on neurons on one side of the synaptic cleft at the dendrites of the neuron. Neurotransmitters that are waiting on the other side either fit into the receptors and so cross the gap, or do not fit and so are released into the gap, which means that uptake is blocked.

Reductionist approach a search for facts that looks at parts in order to draw conclusions rather than studying the whole (which would be a holistic approach). For example, looking at which parts of the brain are activated when someone is talking is a reductionist approach because it looks only at brain activity, whereas taking account of what is being said and why, as well as how other decisions are made and who is speaking, would be a holistic approach.

Reuptake neurotransmitter in the synpatic gap that has not been received by receptors of the post-synaptic neuron is taken back up by the post-synaptic neuron for reuse.

Sampling in a study rarely can all the relevant people be involved so a sample is taken, to represent the whole target population.

Scatter diagram a graph used for correlation data where each point on the graph represents one person's score on two scales. This is the only time a scattergraph should be used to represent data. A line of best fit can show if there is a correlation or not, prior to carrying out a statistical test.

Secondary data data gathered by someone else.

Sense check looking at scores to see if they seem significant in terms of difference or relationship, or not.

Strength of a correlation a correlation that is close to perfect (+1 for a positive correlation and −1 for a negative correlation) is a strong one.

Strong correlation close to perfect correlation.

Superego the third part of the personality, which works on the morality principle. It is made up of the conscience, which is given by parents and society, and the ego ideal, which is the person the individual thinks they should be.

Synapse the gap between the dendrites of one neuron and the axon terminal of another neuron. Whether or not the neurotransmitter produced passes across the gap to the receptors waiting for it decides whether a message passes on or is blocked.

Terminal buttons at the end of the axon of a neuron, where chemicals are released.

Thanatos the death instinct, which is the ultimate way to reduce the arousal of the life instinct.

Twin studies comparisons of MZ and DZ twins on certain characteristics to see if there are differences between how frequently the MZ twins and how frequently the DZ twins share the characteristic. If there are quite strong differences then that characteristic is said to have a genetic basis, at least to an extent.

Unconscious mind the part of the mind that according to Freud is hidden so that we cannot access it. It holds thoughts and feelings that have a strong effect on our behaviour and our lives. Sometimes that effect is negative, but if such unconscious thoughts are made conscious, their negative effect is removed.

The learning approach

Behaviour modification in operant conditioning by using various schedules of reinforcement and patterns of rewards and punishments, behaviour can be modified. One way of doing this is shaping.

Conditioned response (CR) in classical conditioning, the reflex or involuntary response that has been conditioned to occur to a specific stimulus that would not usually elicit that response. The specific stimulus (the conditioned/ neutral stimulus) has to be paired with an unconditioned stimulus to get the required response, and only when that conditioned stimulus on its own gets the response is the response called a conditioned response. In Pavlov's experiments one conditioned response is salivation to a bell.

Conditioned stimulus (CS) in classical conditioning, the specific stimulus that is deliberately paired with an unconditioned stimulus so that eventually the conditioned stimulus alone gets the response, which is then called a conditioned response. In Pavlov's experiments, one conditioned stimulus (the neutral stimulus before it is paired) is a bell.

Content analysis a method used to analyse written data or data from drawings. Data from documents, tapes, drawings and so on are considered to find instances of key terms, for example.

Controls science requires firm data that are reliable and objective. To draw firm conclusions studies need to use controls carefully, to avoid bias.

Conventional content analysis picking categories out from the data (such as looking to see how mental health is mentioned in the media and generating categories) but without theory in mind.

Covert with the observation being done secretly so that the participants do not know that it is taking place.

Critical values tables tables of figures against which the results of a statistical test are checked for significance. There are special tables for each test.

Degrees of freedom (df) the number of cells in a table that are free to vary if the column and the row totals are known.

Directive content analysis is where theory drives the categories (e.g. looking for right-wing authoritarian traits).

Ecological validity the extent to which the setting of a study is real life, so that data are real and the study is (with regard to the setting at least) gathering the data it is claiming to gather.

Empiricism the idea that knowledge comes only from sense data. Empirical data are data collected by sight, sound, taste, smell and touch. Science uses empirical data to test hypotheses that are derived from theories.

Ethics principles that must be adhered to in a psychology study, given by bodies such as the British Psychological Society or, for animals, the Animals (Scientific Procedures) Act, 1986.

Event sampling choosing what to observe and then making notes or tallying each time that event happens.

Extinction in classical conditioning, when a previously conditioned response to a conditioned stimulus no longer occurs because the pairing of the unconditioned stimulus with the conditioned stimulus to get the association no longer occurs.

Falsification looking at a claim (hypothesis) to see if it can be shown not to be the case. For example we can find helpful females many times but we cannot say all females are helpful. When we find one unhelpful female we can show the opposite is the case (not all females are helpful) — we can falsify but not prove.

Generalisability the sample is such that results can be said to be true for the target population.

Imitation one of the processes of observational learning, in social learning theory. Once behaviour has been modelled, it is imitated, depending on certain circumstances such as the observed consequences of the behaviour for the model.

Inferential statistics tests to see whether variables being studied are different or related enough to draw conclusions to that effect. Tests include the Spearman, Wilcoxon, Mann–Whitney U, and Chi-squared.

Internal validity any cause-and-effect conclusion drawn from a study is acceptable, in that there is no bias that might affect such a conclusion, and no other 'cause'. As there is not likely to be 'no' bias, it is the degree of internal validity that is important — a study needs as much as possible.

Index